BASIC

CANTONESE COOKING

JAMES ROLLBAND

BESS PRESS
HONOLULU, HAWAII

Cover art by Jason Teraoka

Cover design by Paula Newcomb

Illustrations by Raymond Larrett

Drawing on page 74 by J. Pryor

Rollband, James
Basic Cantonese Cooking
Honolulu, Hawaii: The Bess Press, Inc.
224 pages

Library of Congress Catalog Card Number: 76-17271

ISBN: 1-880188-45-7

This book was formerly published under the title
The Long and The Short of Chinese Cooking

Dedicated to my parents.
They know why.

Contents

Introduction

My earliest memory of eating Chinese food was when I was five years old. My father had done some work for a Chinese restaurant at the New York World's Fair and he took us along one Sunday afternoon when he went to get paid. The weather was good and we sat at a long table in a tent which was open at all sides. My father told the waiter that I liked chicken wings. I don't remember much about that day--I do remember being served the largest plate of chicken wings I ever saw.

My father was a metal worker, an expert in heating and ventilating systems. He had a good reputation in the Chinese community and did a great deal of work for them. Over the years, he took me with him on a variety of jobs. While he worked, I quietly observed the chefs at their ranges. When I was about eighteen, it suddenly struck me that they were organizing the food in a pattern which was unfamiliar to me. When a chef received an order say for "Shrimp with Bean Sprouts," he would take two pots to the refrigerator and fill one with shrimp and wood ears and the other with bean sprouts. As for the spices and fluid ingredients, he grouped these near the stove. On a tray stood salt, pepper, soy sauce, sherry, garlic, ginger, molasses, black beans, oyster sauce, and sesame oil. On the stove was a pot of soup stock. Nearby was a bowl of corn starch dissolved in water. When a chef began to cook, he would dip the ladle into the stock, place the condiments on top of the stock (still in the ladle), stir the mixture, and then pour the contents of the ladle into the wok. If he needed more fluids later on, he would repeat the process.

I translated this utilitarian arrangement of pots and ladles into a home arrangement of plates and cups. If a chef used two pots, I called them plate 1 and plate 2. The first time he used the ladle, I called it cup 1, the second time cup 2, and so on. This arrangement of plates and cups became the basis of my simplified method of Chinese cooking which brings Chinese restaurant cooking into the home. Chinese cooking does not have to be a subtle and mysterious gourmet skill. It can be truly easy--can give you delicious meals in a short space of time. It all depends on your cooking methods and on your preparation techniques.

What takes longest in cooking a Chinese meal is the preparation, the cutting and chopping that must go on before a meal. But this cutting and chopping can be done ahead of time so that it is easy to proceed. The meat and fish can be purchased fresh, boned if necessary, cut in 4 oz. or 8 oz. portions, frozen flat, packaged individually. Just before a meal, a portion can be taken out of the freezer, thawed for 20 minutes and sliced thinly while it is still firm.

A bottle of soup stock can be kept in the refrigerator at all times, either made the long way or the short way with bouillon cubes. Garlic can be kept minced in a jar covered with peanut oil. Fresh ginger can be kept minced in a jar covered with dry sherry. Corn starch can be kept dissolved in water in a cup or pitcher in the refrigerator. Enough rice can be cooked at one time so that there is enough left over to cook several more meals. And if you do sufficient cooking, you can keep a container of minced onions and other frequently used vegetables in your refrigerator.

You can prepare a meal in minutes this way. And you can also expand a meal quickly for unexpected guests. Suppose you made Shrimp with Bean Sprouts for yourself, and two friends arrived from out of town. Cover the finished dish and cut up one onion into wedges and cut 4 stalks of celery in diagonal pieces 1/2" wide. Heat 1 tablespoon oil in a wok, add 1/2 teaspoon salt, and stir fry the vegetables 1 minute over medium heat. Add 1/4 cup chicken stock and simmer with a cover 3 minutes. Then add the dish you had prepared for yourself and stir. No extra dishes were prepared but vegetables were added to build up the volume of the Shrimp with Vegetables so you could feed 2 extra people. On another occasion, you might want to try canned mushrooms, frozen peas, canned bamboo shoots and water chestnuts. Once you start cooking this way, improvising will be easy.

I have not indicated the number of servings for each recipe. In Chinese cooking, one dish equals one serving. If you are preparing dinner for five people, prepare five dishes, not counting soup or rice. If the people are not very hungry, you can cut down the number of main dishes. Just use your judgment.

To sum up, there are several advantages to cooking Chinese style. It is a great cuisine, comparable to the French. It is simple to master. It is economical since it uses small quantities of meat or fish. It looks good on a plate because the vegetables are cooked swiftly and retain their bright colors. It tastes good because the food retains its nutrients.

KITCHEN EQUIPMENT

Stoves

A Chinese restaurant stove delivers 125,000 BTU whereas the home stove delivers only 6,500 to 15,000. This means a chef can cook Lobster Cantonese in 1-2 minutes while it will take a home cook 8-10 minutes to do the same job. Moreover, the restaurant stove is more flexible in that each unit has 2-3 burners which can be adjusted individually.

A home cook, however, can learn to cook well on an ordinary stove. If there is a choice, get a gas stove, not an electric one. When you work with gas, you can vary the heat by turning the dial delicately. When you work with electrical units, only three or four variations are possible on a dial. Then too, they are somewhat sluggish in response, taking a few minutes to heat up and a few minutes to cool down.

If you have no choice and must use an electric stove, don't use a wok at all. It is designed specifically for gas heat, where the flames rise in an arc to embrace the round bottom. Instead, use a flat bottom pan (like a 10" chicken fryer with a tight-fitting cover) which will sit snugly on the heating unit. And to make up for the sluggishness of an electric stove's responses, you may have to keep one burner on high and another on low and shift the pan from one to the other--Chinese cooking requires a quick eye and an ever-varying temperature.

Wok

The most basic kitchen tool, the wok can be used to feed one person or ten. Because of the round bottom which cooks food evenly, the wok handles one cup of food as well as it handles ten.

Size: buy a 14" size to begin with and then, if you wish, buy a smaller wok and a larger wok.

Material: buy an iron or steel wok. Stainless steel is all right for soups or sweet-sour dishes. It is really no good for stir frying because it develops hot spots and can't be seasoned properly. Aluminum is too soft a metal for woks.

Kind: buy one with a wooden handle on the side if you can. They are very useful--you can lift the wok with one hand and stir food inside with the other. You can also empty a wok more quickly.

When you buy a wok, it will have a protective coating or lacquer on it to prevent rust. Scrub this with steel-wool and scouring powder to get the coating off. Dry with a paper towel. Pour a few drops of peanut oil in the wok. Heat the oil, spread it around with a paper towel until the inside of the wok is coated Continue heating the wok until the oil smokes and the wok begins to turn black Don't worry about appearances--the black coating will prevent food from sticking.

After the wok has been used, clean it this way. Put 1 cup of water in the wok and heat to boiling. Move the water around with a wok brush or any small brush to loosen any stuck food, pour out the water, rinse the wok, then heat and repeat oil and paper towel seasoning procedure. If necessary, wash the wok with water and scour with plastic scouring pad, and when clean, season. The point is to be careful not to scratch the inside surface of the wok.

Wok Ring

Do not use a wok without a ring which is necessary to stabilize
the wok on the stove. It is usually made from galvanized steel
or aluminum; either is fine. Make sure the bottom of the ring is
large enough to rest on the top of the stove. If you have a stove
which requires a special size ring, go to your local sheet-metal
shop and have a ring made. It will cost a few dollars, but it's
well worth the money.

Wok Cover

You should buy a cover when you buy a wok. It is absolutely
essential to cover food at times when you are stir frying. Also,
a cover enables you to steam various dishes. Buy one 1/2" to 1"
smaller than the wok to keep the condensation (which forms
inside the cover and drips down) inside the wok, not on the
stove. Get as deep a cover as possible to give you flexibility in
steaming.

Wok Turner

Unlike a spatula which is flat, the turner is curved. When the turner is held in a horizontal position 2" from bottom of wok, it should fit the contours of the wok perfectly. If the turner has a rough edge (feel it with your finger), file it down and use emery paper to smooth it. The point is not to scratch the inside surface of the wok in any way. If you can, buy a turner made of stainless steel—they last much longer.

Ladle

These come in different sizes. Buy the 1 cup size to begin with. The ladle is extraordinarily useful. You can empty a wok with it, drain oil and so on. You can also use a 4" ladle as a very small wok, to make miniature egg turnovers or small egg foo youngs.

Soup Pot

You should buy one with a close fitting cover, large enough to hold a 5-6 lb. chicken or duck with room to spare. Either buy an enamel one generally used for boiling lobsters, or a stainless steel 12 quart job. A stainless steel pot will cost a great deal of money but will last forever.

Chinese Steamer

Bamboo is generally preferred because it doesn't transfer the heat as rapidly as aluminum ones. See the Rice Chapter for a drawing of a bamboo steamer. These are intended to be used in a wok or large pot. They are strong and with normal care will last a long time. They come very small or very big. Buy one that will fit inside your wok. Aluminum steamers have trays and a top and bottom section. Some are big enough to hold a whole duck. There is a small gadget sold in gourmet stores which you might find useful; it signals when the water in steamers is very low—it looks like a pot cover with a rim on both sides.

You can use a wok to steam food. A stainless steel one is best. Otherwise, the steaming will remove the treasured oil film on the surface of your other woks. Place a trivet or two pieces of wood on the bottom of the wok; chopsticks will work fine, or an empty tuna-fish can. Punch two small holes in the side of the can, one near the top, one near the bottom to prevent the plate you are steaming from being lifted by the steam. Fill the wok with water within 1" of the top of the can. Put plate with food you are steaming on the can. Place cover on wok and proceed.

Hot Plate Lifter

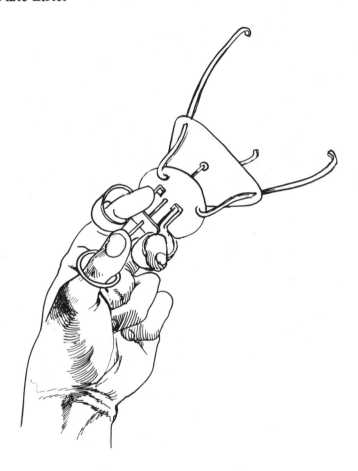

The hot plate lifter was invented to lift plates of food from the steamer. It looks like a tripod with a ring on top with hooks on the bottom. This is a very handy gadget.

Cleavers

There are a few styles which I prefer, usually made from stainless steel or high carbon steel. Stainless steel ones don't discolor. High carbon steel will--you will have to wipe it after each use. But high carbon steel will hold an edge longer.

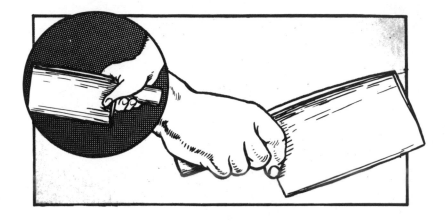

The first and most used cleaver is the slicing knife, about 3 1/2" high by 8" long. The top of the knife is 1/8" tapering gradually to the edge. The handle is wooden. It can be used to slice vegetables, fish, and meat. Hold the knife in the right hand with the thumb on one side of the blade and the first finger on the other side of the blade. See diagram. The left hand holds the food to be cut. The knife rests on the knuckle or flat part of the finger between the first and second joint, depending on the height of what is being cut. The blade is never lifted more than 1/8" above the food that is being cut--this method protects the fingers. The cutting stroke is forward, and after each cut the left hand is moved back the width of the cut. This cleaver should never be used to cut bones. When you use it correctly, it is totally safe.

I prefer to have my butcher cut apart bones for me, using a bandsaw; so I don't use the chopping cleaver very often.

Boning Knife

A narrow boning knife is handy for separating chicken bones at the joint.

Miscellany

You will need a small scale which measures weight accurately in ounces. You will also need measuring spoons and cups—Pyrex 2 and 4 cup measuring cups with pouring lips are extremely useful. So are plastic containers for storing dry items. They prevent larder beetles from getting into noodles and grains.

COOKING METHODS

Chow or Stir Frying

This is a basic Chinese style of cooking, similar to shallow frying or sautéing. It was designed to save fuel which was and is expensive in China. By cutting food into small pieces and stirring it at high heat, a minimum quantity of fuel is used.

First the wok is heated. Then oil is added and salt (which prevents spattering). Then the minced garlic is put in the wok. When the garlic is the proper golden color, the main ingredients are placed in the wok and constantly stirred until almost done. The sauce is added, the mixture is stirred and everything is ready at the same time.

Deep Fat Frying

The wok is the best designed utensil for deep frying. Never fill it more than one-half to three-quarters full. When the oil expands, the outward curve of the wok will give it plenty of room.

There is a Japanese tempura pan which is also good for deep frying. It has two strainers, one to hold the fried food until the excess oil drains off, the other to skim the oil particles near the surface and at the bottom of the pan.

After you are finished deep frying, you will want to strain the oil to use it again. Get an old drip coffee-pot at a rummage sale. Put a coffee filter or paper towel into the drip basket and pour used oil into the top of the pot. It will drip through. The paper will catch the small particles and the top container will filter any large particles.

Boiling

Not quite the same as our cooking, Chinese chefs use this as an intermediate, not a final step in cooking. Chicken, for instance, is cooked very briefly before it is smoked. Boiling time, except for soup, is very brief.

Red Cooking

Soy Sauce added to boiling liquid gives the food a red color.

Steaming

This is one of my favorite methods. It is difficult to make mistakes with steaming, and the food tastes very good because none of the nutrients boil away. If you have a few trays in your steamers, several dishes can be prepared at one time. Corn, clams and other non-oriental foods can be steamed with ease. Try a steamer and you will wonder how you ever got along without one. See the discussion earlier in the Introduction on steamers.

Roasting

This method is used for pork and for spareribs. It is similar to our roasting, except Chinese cooks marinate the meat before putting it in the oven, so that the flavor does not remain on the surface but penetrates completely. While baking, the meat is basted frequently with the marinade to keep the surface from drying out. The outside of the meat will thus have a nice color. Water is placed in a pan at the bottom of the oven to prevent the meat from drying out and to keep the grease drippings from catching fire.

Smoking

This is a finishing process to flavor food. It will convert an ordinary steamed chicken into a classic dish, merely by burning tea and brown sugar. You can buy a smoking oven from sporting-goods houses. These have a small electric plate at the bottom with a small tray above of hickory chips soaked in water to slow the burning rate. You can blend several kinds of wood chips for different flavors. If you wish to pursue smoking further, there are good books available.

INGREDIENTS FOR CHINESE COOKING

Bamboo Shoots

Available in cans from 4 ounces to 5 lbs. When the can is opened, the shoots should be rinsed in cold water and cut to size. The shoots not used immediately should be stored covered with water in the refrigerator. If the water is changed every other day, the shoots will last about one week.

Bean Curd (To Fu)

Made from soybeans. Available in a cake or piece. This is not easy to make at home, though some people do. It is available commercially at low cost and can be stored for about a week if it is kept covered in water in the refrigerator and the water is changed every day. Bean curd has no flavor of its own but picks up the flavor of the foods it is mixed with. It can be fried, deep fried, boiled or steamed. It also can be sliced as is and served with any sauce.

Bean curd is one of the most important staples in Chinese home cooking. Once you start using it, you will not be able to cook without it but will look for recipes for it. If fresh bean curd is not available, canned can be used instead. It is firmer and for stir fry dishes an improvement over the fresh curd because it won't fall apart in the wok.

Bean Sprouts

These are made usually from mung beans. You can buy fresh or canned in grocery stores, or you can sprout them yourself. If you buy them canned, be sure to crisp them in ice water for 30 minutes. If you decide to sprout them at home (it is very easy), soak 1/4 cup mung beans in warm water overnight. Spread a double layer of cheese cloth in the bottom of a plastic colander. Rinse the beans and place them on the cheese cloth. Place a clean towel on top of the colander and sprinkle this with 1 quart water at room temperature. Continue this watering 2 to 3 times a day for four or five days until the sprouts are full grown. If you keep the colander in a dark place like a closet, the sprouts will be whiter. In very warm weather the beans sprout faster, in cold weather more slowly. When the sprouts are mature, dump them into a large pot and fill with water; stir the sprouts until the hulls separate. Most of the hulls will float to the surface and can be scooped out with a slotted spoon or ladle.

There is a still better way to sprout beans. Get 3 cottage cheese containers which are empty. The 5 lb. size is good. Discard the covers. Cut the bottom off one container. Punch holes in the bottom of the other two containers--about sixty 1/16" holes. Be careful to punch holes in the bottom rim. Soak 1/4 cup mung beans in warm water overnight. Rinse these in the morning and place them in one of the containers with the holes. Level the beans with the back of a spoon. Put the other container with holes inside the first container with the beans. Put both containers inside the sleeve, the container without its bottom. Water a minimum of four times a day, more often if you like. The more often you water the beans, the better the sprouts will grow. Keep the contraption on a drainboard in the kitchen, covered with a clean large cloth to keep out light. The container with no bottom holds the beans above the drainboard to help drainage. The container inside the bean container aids watering. In summer the process takes 3-4 days, in winter about 5 days. Separate as above.

Bird's Nest

Used in making soups. This is a swallow's nest made from plants and sea-weed from the sea gathered by the industrious bird. It is expensive, but the taste is worth the money. Some restaurants use the nest in stuffing chicken or duck.

Black Beans

A soy bean which has been fermented. They should be rinsed in a strainer before using and mashed by itself or with garlic. It is used in fish and lobster dishes and for chicken, beef and spareribs. It can be purchased in cans or plastic bags and can be stored in the refrigerator for a long time.

Cellophane Noodles (Long Rice or Chinese Vermicelli)

Made from mung beans. Transparent before being cooked. Can be used for soup or noodle dishes. Can be stir fried or used as topping for dishes like Lobster Soong. When deep fried, it puffs up to several times its volume and becomes porous, enabling it to absorb flavors of surrounding food.

Chinese Cabbage (Bok Choy or Bok Toy)

The stalks are sliced and used in many dishes; the leaves are used in soups. Available in Chinese grocery stores year round, also supermarkets. To store, keep in refrigerator in bucket with 1" water at the bottom. Change water every other day. It will keep a few weeks to a few months. If a brown spot or line forms at the bottom, trim it off with a potato peeler.

Chinese Celery Cabbage (Siu Choy or Tiensin Cabbage)

Similar to Chinese cabbage in shape but the leaves are pale green, not jade green. Available in supermarkets. Can be stored the same as Chinese cabbage.

Chinese Sausage (Lop Chong)

This will keep many months in the refrigerator. It is sweet unlike American sausage. Children love it cut in 1/4" pieces and heated until the fat particles become transparent and served on toothpicks. It can be stir fried, used in dumplings, or steamed with rice.

Corn, Baby

Miniature corn only 3" long in cans. It need only be heated. Many people like it cold in salads. The complete ear is eaten including the cob.

Duck Sauce

A sweet-sour sauce made from plums. It is used as a dip for egg rolls, roast pork, roast duck, etc. However, it is not used in sweet-sour dishes. It will keep well in the refrigerator.

Five Spice (Ng Heung Fun)

A brownish powder containing anise pepper, star anise, fennel, cloves, and cinnamon. It is used in many dishes: roast pork, spareribs, roast duck, etc. It will keep a long time if stored in a cool dark place.

Garlic

This is the one ingredient used most frequently in Chinese dishes, only salt and soy sauce are used more. It is heated in oil first--this causes garlic to lose its aggressive aroma. It becomes mellow but the flavor remains. It can be stored for long periods if needed by mincing a few dozen cloves, then putting them in peanut oil and storing in the refrigerator. When you need garlic, use 1/4-1/8 teaspoon minced garlic in oil from the refrigerator in place of one clove. The amount depends on the size of the garlic you use and the taste. Strangely, garlic varies in taste from strong and sharp to mild and sweet. Try out any new garlic you buy before deciding on quantity to use.

Ginger Root

This looks like a small potato with many arms. Sold by weight in Chinese or Spanish grocery stores; it is increasingly found in supermarkets. To store, peel it with a potato peeler, cut into 1/8" slices and store covered with sherry in a jar with a lid in the refrigerator. It will last many months. Ginger root is also available in cans or crushed dried.

Golden Needles (Tiger Lily)

It comes dried from China and is used in exotic dishes like Moo Shi Pork.

Hoisin Sauce

This is a dark reddish sauce made from soybeans and spices. It is used in cooking and steaming and as a dip for fish and poultry. It is available in cans and jars and can be stored in the refrigerator for a long time.

Hot Stuff

Since Mandarin cooking has become popular, people have wanted to duplicate some of the dishes at home. There are now available some condiments that solve the problem of making hot dishes.

--Tabasco or hot pepper sauce is the easiest to obtain. 1/2 teaspoon is a good starting point for most people and the amount can be increased to taste.

--Cayenne or ground red pepper can also be used. Start with 1/2 teaspoon for most dishes and increase amount to taste.

--Red Pepper Flakes are available in Chinese grocery stores. Since the pieces are larger than ground pepper, you should make certain they are distributed equally throughout the dish. They are hot. Start with 1/2 teaspoon.

--Hot Peppers or chili are available dried in Chinese grocery stores. Four of these can be gently fried in oil for most dishes.

They are extremely hot, so eat them with caution and a glass of water. Fresh hot peppers are harder to find. Two fresh peppers are usually enough for most dishes. Slice them thin and remove seeds which conceal hidden fire of boundless power.

—Chili Sauce is a hot sauce containing garlic, chili, vinegar, sugar, and salt. When you use it, cut down on any seasonings used in a recipe, especially garlic.

—Hot Oil can be made easily at home. Heat 1 cup peanut oil. When it starts to smoke, add 2 tablespoons ground red pepper (cayenne). Let the mixture cool. Then pour through a strainer into a bottle with a tight fitting cap.

Lichee Nuts

These are available dried with a brown paper shell and a large pit or canned with the shell off and the pit removed. Use either for dessert. Use the canned type with chicken, duck or pork. Save the syrup for cooking.

Molasses

Get bead molasses or an unsulphured variety. It is used as a coloring agent and a flavor for dishes like fried rice. Not much is used. Once it is heated, it spreads fast, it will coat the rice and partially seal its surface.

Monosodium Glutamate (MSG or Ac'cent)

This is a powder which brings out the flavor in food. Its use is optional in this book. There has been some controversy on the effect of MSG on the digestive tract. If you plan to use it, add 1/2 teaspoon to any recipe.

Mustard

This is a table dip made from mustard powder and water with a dash of vinegar. It is usually served with egg rolls, spareribs, etc.

Mushrooms, Black

Available in dried form. Before using they should be soaked in warm water for 15-30 minutes. The water can be saved for use in soup or sauces if desired. The mushrooms are drained and excess water squeezed out, stems removed and mushrooms cut to correct size.

Mushrooms, Straw

Available canned or dried; they are white and brown or grey-colored.

Oyster Sauce

This is a dark brown sauce made from cooking oysters with soy sauce and spices. It is available in jars and cans. Once opened, it can be kept in the refrigerator for a long time.

Peanut Oil

This is the primary Chinese cooking oil because it can be brought to a high temperature without smoking. It can be used for deep fat frying or stir frying. After a few days use, filter the oil through paper filters. These are low priced and readily available, but if you can't find any, fold a white paper towel to fit a one quart funnel, or press the center of the towel into the funnel until it almost reaches the hole. Put two spring-type clothespins on the top to hold the towel. When the oil has cooled to room temperature, pour it into the funnel which has been placed in a storage jar. The oil will drip through in 6 hours. Store in refrigerator.

Chinese chefs like to flavor foods with oil which has been used for previous frying. Some fry fish or shrimp in deep fat and use the oil for flavoring some other dish.

Rice Noodles or Rice Sticks

One of the best tasting noodles in a Chinese store. It is available fresh or dried.

Sesame Oil

A light colored oil used for flavoring. A few drops are used in soups or stir frying when the dish is almost ready to be used.

Sherry

Use the New York State sherry (Taylors or Widmers are fine). Do not use cooking sherry since it contains salt and is more expensive than sherry bought in a liquor store.

Shrimp Chips

Used as an appetizer or decoration on a serving tray. Made from shrimps and a starch.

Snow Peas or Sugar Peas

These are flat and have small peas in the pod. They range from 2-4 inches. The ends are snapped off and the string on the outside is removed if it is coarse. Since they are expensive, only a few are used in a dish. They are in season in early summer (like regular peas) and are also available frozen in supermarkets. They are added to the dish very late, so that they do not cook more than 2-4 minutes.

Soy Sauce

American types are usually salt water with flavor and color added. The Japanese types available in the U.S. (Kikkoman) are excellent. They are made by heating water, salt and soybeans.The mixture is strained and then aged 12-18 months.

Soy Sauce (Thick or Heavy)

This is regular soy sauce mixed one to one with molasses. It is available in jars or cans.

Star Anise

A small brown star with 8 points. It can be broken into the individual points for cooking and tied in cheesecloth for easy removal before serving. When you purchase star anise in a Chinese grocery store, you will usually be given a small bag of anise pepper tc go with the star anise. Use one pepper bud along with one anise point.

Vinegar

Rice or Wine types are o.k. for Chinese cooking. Cider vinegar is also all right.

Water Chestnuts

These have a crispy, crunchy texture with no particular flavor. Used in steamed and stir fried dishes, they can also be served cold in salads. Chestnuts are available in cans. Place in a container and cover with water. If you change the water every day, they will last a week or more.

Water Chestnut Powder (or flour)

Used as a thickening powder like cornstarch, but more expensive. Also used with flour or cornstarch to make a better and more stable batter, or by itself for the best batter for exotic dishes, like Wor Shu Op.

Wood Ears (Wun Yee)

It is a fungus and must be soaked in water 15-30 minutes before using. It will expand many times its size. When soaked, run your fingers over them to pick out the hard stems.

Yee Fu Mein

This is a Japanese noodle which is very convenient. It cooks in four minutes in boiling water.

Yellow Fish

Now available frozen from China. The best tasting fish you ever had. Used in Sweet and Sour and Fried dishes.

Menus

Most Chinese restaurants serve meals family style—platters are placed in the center of the table and guests serve themselves. The virtue of this system is that many dishes can be sampled at one sitting. But people don't always take advantage of the system. It is sad to watch a party of six people come into a restaurant and order three Chicken Chow Meins, two Pork Chow Meins, and one Shrimp Chow Mein. These six dishes are basically the same, with different toppings.

To get a variety of textures and tastes, you should order dishes prepared in different ways, some stir fried, some deep fat fried, some steamed. You should also order dishes made with different meats and fish.

For five people, you will want five main courses. You can adjust this figure upwards or downwards, depending on the appetites of the people involved. Here is a sample menu for five. Five main courses: Shrimp with Lobster Sauce, Pepper Steak, Pork Egg Foo Yong, Sweet and Sour Fish Slices, and Lemon Chicken. These main dishes would be accompanied by a soup— Egg Drop or Won Ton, an appetizer—Egg Rolls or Barbequed Spare Ribs, boiled rice, tea, and a dessert—Almond Cookies.

When planning a meal at home, the problem is a little more difficult since the equipment and work space will be limited. You will have to limit the number of dishes accordingly; two or three of the main dishes should be dropped and the remaining ones doubled or tripled so that there will be enough to eat. The trick is to maintain sufficient variety so that the meal remains interesting.

At home it is easiest for the cook to prepare ahead of time and finish up at the last moment. Soup can be made earlier and kept warm on the back of the stove at low heat. The barbequed spare ribs can be baked in the oven at an early time also. Then the main dishes can be cooked quickly one at a time and kept warm in a 175 degree oven. All the dishes can be brought to the table at the same time this way.

Begin with only two main dishes, doubling or tripling the quantity of ingredients as necessary. When the process becomes simple, increase the number of main dishes as you wish.

MENUS FOR 2
Boiled rice & tea are served with all meals.

Chicken Corn Soup
Roast Pork
Yellow Fish
Chinese Roast Lamb
Almond Fruit Gelatin

Tomato Egg Drop Soup
Rumaki
Lobster Cantonese
Roast Pork Lo Mein
Ice Cream

Chinese Vegetable Soup
Chicken Wings, Red Cooked
Wor Shu Op
Beef with String Beans
Bananas in Honey

Won Ton Soup
Barbequed Spareribs
Shrimp with Lobster Sauce
Fried Rice
Chinese Sponge Cake

Watercress with Pork Soup
Crispy Chicken Wings
Pepper Steak
Shrimp Lo Mein
Honey Apples

Egg Drop Soup
Egg Rolls (2)
Pineapple Chicken
Almond Cookies

MENUS FOR 4
Boiled rice & tea are served with all meals.

Mushroom Egg Drop Soup	Cellophane Noodle Soup
Egg Rolls (4)	Chicken Wings in Five Spice
Roast Pork with Bean Sprouts	Shrimp with Bean Sprouts
Shrimp Egg Foo Young	Cabbage, Bacon & Oyster Sauce
Curried Chicken	Beef with Cucumbers
Jello	Chilled Lichee Nuts (Canned)

Won Ton Soup	Chicken Corn Soup
Egg Rolls (4)	Barbequed Spareribs
Smoked Chicken	Lemon Chicken
Lobster Cantonese	Shrimp in Lobster Sauce
Beef with String Beans	Beef with Peas
Roast Pork Fried Rice	Lamb with Scallions
Almond Cookies	Honey Apples

Leek & Mushroom Soup	Birds Nest Soup
Chicken Wings in Oyster Sauce	Roast Pork
Stir Fried Ground Beef	Chicken in Tomato Sauce
Steamed Lobster	Beef with Asparagus
Lamb with Scallions	Shrimp Lo Mein
Moo Shi Pork	Sweet & Sour Vegetables
Chinese Sponge Cake	Fruit Cocktail

MENUS FOR 6
Boiled rice & tea are served with all meals.

Won Ton Soup	Egg Drop Soup
Crispy Chicken Wings	Egg Rolls (6)
Shrimp with Bean Sprouts	Bamboo Shoots with Mushrooms
Pepper Steak	Beef with Cellophane Noodles
Moo Shi Pork	Roast Pork with Bean Sprouts
Cabbage, Bacon & Oyster Sauce	Peking Duck
Wor Shu Op	Sweet & Sour Fish Slices
Lobster Cantonese	Golden Chicken
Almond Cookies	Fortune Cookies

Tomato Egg Drop Soup	Leek & Mushroom Soup
Shrimp Toast	Shrimp Balls
Smoked Chicken	Peking Duck
Spareribs with Pineapple	Chicken with Cashews
Stir Fried Fresh Asparagus	Yellow Fish
Roast Pork with Bean Sprouts	Ham Fried Rice
Lobster Cantonese	Stir Fried Ground Beef
Beef with Broccoli	Lamb with Scallions
Almond Fruit Gelatin	Chinese Sponge Cake

Hot & Sour Soup	Birds Nest Soup
Egg Rolls (6)	Barbequed Spare Ribs
Fried Lemon Chicken	Stir Fried Celery
Roast Pork Lo Mein	Pineapple Chicken
Beef with Cucumbers	Beef with Cellophane Noodles
Steamed Lobster	Sweet & Sour Fish (whole)
Stir Fried Broccoli	Shrimp in Lobster Sauce
Shrimp Fried Rice	Twice Cooked Pork
Almond Cookies	Jello

MENUS FOR 8
Boiled rice & tea are served with all meals.

Egg Drop Soup
Shrimp Balls
Chinese Roast Lamb
Pineapple Chicken
Beef with String Beans
Stir Fried Asparagus
Wor Shu Op
Pork with Cellophane Noodles
Steamed Lobster
Stir Fried Bean Sprouts
Ice Cream

Leek and Mushroom Soup
Barbequed Spareribs
Shrimp with Bean Sprouts
Roast Pork Lo Mein
Lobster Cantonese
Chicken with Mushrooms
Roast Pork Fried Rice
Pineapple Duck
Beef with Cucumbers
Stir Fried Lettuce
Jello

Won Ton Soup
Egg Rolls
Stir Fried Asparagus
Shrimp with Bean Sprouts
Shredded Beef, Chili Peppers
Chicken with Mushrooms
Boneless Pressed Duck
Yellow Fish
Lobster Cantonese
Roast Pork Fried Rice
Sherbet

Tomato Egg Drop Soup
Chicken Wings in Oyster Sauce
Stir Fried Broccoli
Sweet and Sour Carrots
Cabbage Bacon and Oyster Sauce
Chicken in Tomato Sauce
Pepper Steak
Boneless Pressed Duck
Shrimp in Lobster Sauce
Roast Pork Egg Foo Young
Chinese Sponge Cake

Hot and Sour Soup
Fried Won Tons
Bamboo Shoots, Mushrooms
Bean Curd, Black Beans, Garlic
Lobster Cantonese
Chicken with Cashews
Beef with Cellophane Noodles
Pineapple Duck
Ham Fried Rice
Shrimp with Vegetables
Almond Fruit Gelatin

Cellophane Noodle Soup
Crispy Chicken Wings
Sweet and Sour Fish Slices
Chicken with Mushrooms
Pepper Steak
Peking Duck
Pork with Cellophane Noodles
Lobster Soong
Lamb with Vegetables
Stir Fried Celery
Almond Cookies

Tea

You begin a Chinese meal with tea. All teas come from the same plant, but there is a basic difference between green and black tea. In green tea, the better leaves are chosen because they retain their appearance in the final product. The leaves are dried as soon as they are picked. Gon Jim is a popular green variety.

Black tea, on the other hand, is fermented first and then dried. Fragrant and strong, Oolong tea has become known as "the Chinese restaurant tea."

Some mixed teas are a blend of black and green. Some contain buds from other plants added for scent and flavor. Lichee and jasmine are the most popular added ingredients.

The Chinese drink their tea without sugar, milk, or lemon. Once you get used to tea served like this, you will like its pure flavor.

Tea should be made in a teapot. Into a ceramic pot (which holds heat), put one teaspoon of tea per cup. Pour on the boiling water. Let steep 3-5 minutes, and your tea is ready.

When the tea is almost gone, refill with boiling water and let this infusion steep about eight minutes. There are those who say the second pot is even better than the first. With some teas, a third infusion is possible.

If the teapot has a center cylinder to hold the tea, or if you use a tea ball, sieve, or basket, remove the leaves after each steeping as soon as the tea reaches the strength you want.

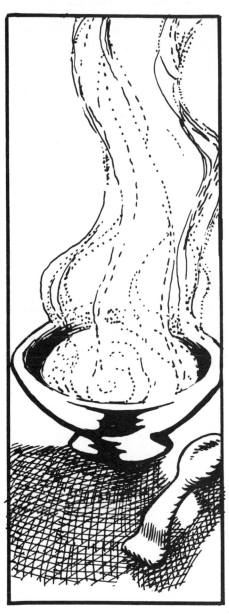

Soup

Before, after, or during meals, soup is a good idea. Soup and tea may be served at social gatherings, with a plate full of fried noodles or egg roll skins, cut into large pieces and deep fried. With heavy meals, a clear soup is best. Jook, which is listed in the Rice Chapter, is very useful. It should not be forgotten when planning a menu.

Porcelain spoons are better than metal spoons for soup. They won't burn your lips because they don't conduct the heat.

In Chinese restaurants, there is always a pot of soup on the stove, set between the woks. Chicken and pork bones are placed in a stainless steel basket and lowered into the pot. Lacking such a basket, some chefs tie the bones or a whole stewing chicken with butcher cord and lower it into the pot for a few hours. When the fat is skimmed off, the stock is ready. Because the pot never boils, the stock remains clear.

BASIC CHICKEN STOCK OR SOUP

1 stewing chicken, about 4 lbs.
2 quarts water
1 slice ginger root 1/8" thick

Clean the chicken and remove as much fat as possible.
Save the liver and giblets for other dishes.
Add the ginger root and water. Bring to a boil.
Then simmer, with a cover, for 15 minutes. Skim off fat.
Cover and let simmer for 1-1/2 hours.
Remove chicken. It can be served hot as is or kept in the
refrigerator for use in other dishes, including Chinese Fried
Chicken. (Consult Index for page number.)
Cool the stock and skim the fat off the top. Strain.
What you do not need immediately, freeze.

BASIC ECONOMY CHICKEN STOCK

2 lbs chicken backs and necks
1 lb. pork bones
2 quarts water
1 slice ginger root, 1/8" thick

Bring to a boil. Cover and simmer 15 minutes. Skim fat off.
Return to stove and simmer, covered, 1-1/2 hours.
Remove chicken parts and pork bones.
Cool the stock and skim fat off top. Strain.
Freeze.

LIGHTNING CHICKEN STOCK

3 cups water
3 envelopes MBT Chicken Bouillon

Mix in bottle and store in refrigerator until needed.

GIBLETS & RICE SOUP
Gai Kan Fan Tong

4 cups water
8 oz. chicken giblets & hearts sliced 1/8" thick
1/3 cup uncooked rice, washed to remove starch
1 medium onion (6 oz.) sliced 1/8" thick
4 oz. mushrooms, stems & pieces
1/4 cup water
1 tablespoon dry sherry
1 teaspoon soy sauce

Bring water and giblets to a boil. Cook for 5 minutes. Remove foam with slotted spoon.
Add rice, onions, and mushrooms. Bring to a boil. Simmer, covered for 20 minutes.
Add the 1/4 cup water, sherry, and soy sauce. Stir and cook 1 minute. Let set for 2-3 minutes.

CHICKEN CORN SOUP
Gai Shok Me Tong

4 cups chicken stock
1/2 cup raw chicken minced fine
1 cup creamed corn
1 slice boiled or Virginia ham chopped fine
2 beaten eggs
1 tablespoon dry sherry

Bring the chicken and stock to a boil. Simmer 10 minutes covered. Add the corn and ham. Bring to a boil and simmer, covered, for 5 minutes. Add the eggs and sherry slowly and stir with chopstick to make threads. Let stand 2 minutes until egg threads firm.

CHICKEN & RICE SOUP, LONG METHOD
Gai Fan Tong

4 cups water
1 giblet diced
1 heart diced
1/2 cup uncooked chicken diced
1/3 cup uncooked rice, washed to remove starch
2 oz. onion coarse chopped
1 teaspoon soy sauce

Bring the water, giblet and heart to a boil. Cover and simmer for
5 minutes. Remove foam with slotted spoon.
Add the chicken, rice, onion and soy sauce. Cover and cook at
medium heat for 20 minutes. Check seasoning.

QUICK CHICKEN & RICE SOUP
Gai Fan Tong

4 cups chicken stock
1 cup leftover rice
1/2 cup cooked chicken cut in matchstick strips
2 oz. onion cut in tangerine size wedges
1 teaspoon soy sauce

Heat until hot, 10-15 minutes. Do not boil.

Won
Ton

WON TON SOUP
Won Ton Tong

Won Tons
1 lb. won ton skins (about 60-80 won tons)
1 lb. ground raw pork
1/2 teaspoon salt
1 teaspoon soy sauce
1 teaspoon sesame oil
1/2 teaspoon corn starch
1/2 teaspoon sugar
1 oz. onion minced fine
3-4 water chestnuts minced fine
1 oz. bamboo shoots minced fine

Mix pork and the remainder of the ingredients thoroughly. Place 1/2 teaspoon of this filling on one corner of the won ton skin. Fold as shown in sketch and seal corner with a dab of beaten egg.

With a slotted spoon, lower the won tons gently into 3-4 quarts of boiling water. Simmer 15 minutes.The won tons will float when they are done. Be careful to cook them at least 15 minutes to insure proper cooking of the raw pork in the filling. Strain in colander.
Place in soup or freeze in units of 12-16 for future use.

Soup
4 cups chicken stock
1 teaspoon dry sherry
12-16 won tons
roast pork cut in matchsticks
1 scallion cut in 1/4" pieces

Bring the stock and sherry to a boil.
Add the won tons and simmer 5 minutes, covered.
Divide in 4 bowls and garnish with roast pork and scallions.

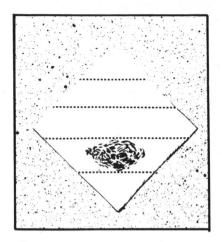

Place drained filling on lower corner of egg roll. Roll up.

Fold inwards on dotted lines.

Pinch corners together, like the top of a bag. Seal with a bit of beaten egg.

FOLDING THE WON TON

CELLOPHANE NOODLE SOUP
Fun See Tong

4 cups chicken stock
4 oz. uncooked chicken in 1/8"x1"x1" pieces
1 teaspoon soy sauce
2 tablespoons corn starch
1/4 teaspoon sesame oil
2 egg whites
4 oz. Virginia ham, sliced 1/8"x1/8"x2"
4 oz. cellophane noodles soaked in warm water 20 minutes, drained and cut in 2" pieces

Bring the chicken stock, chicken, soy sauce, corn starch, and sesame oil to a boil. Cover and simmer 20 minutes.
Add the egg whites. Stir rapidly with a chopstick to break the egg whites into shreds.
Add the ham and cellophane noodles. Stir. Remove from stove and let stand for 5 minutes.

Note: More ingredients can be added to the soup, if it will be the main dish of the meal. A good combination to add, at the time you add the ham and noodles, is the following:
6 snow peas, remove stems
1 piece celery cut in 2" pieces, then in 1/8" strips
1 leaf lettuce cut in 1/8" shreds

EGG DROP SOUP
Dan Far Tong

4 cups chicken stock
2 tablespoons corn starch
1/4 teaspoon salt
3 drops sesame oil
1/4 teaspoon soy sauce
1 slice onion minced fine
1 egg lightly beaten

When mixture starts to boil, add the egg and stir with a fork
to break the egg into shreds. Turn off heat once the egg is set,
about 1-2 minutes.

Variations
Chicken Egg Drop Soup, *Don Far Gai Tong* —
Add 2 tablespoons cooked minced chicken once soup is done.

Mushroom Egg Drop Soup, *Moo Goo Dan Far Tong* —
Add 4 small sliced white mushrooms or 1 oz. canned mushrooms.

Tomato Egg Drop Soup, *Don Far Kair Gai Tong* —
Add 1/2 cup chopped fresh tomato before cooking.

WATERCRESS SOUP
Sai Yong Choy Tong

4 cups stock, chicken or vegetable
1/2 lb. watercress washed and cut in 2" pieces

Bring the stock to a boil. Add the watercress. Cover and simmer
for 5 minutes.

Poached eggs are a nice addition to this recipe. Simply poach
4 eggs and place one on top of each bowl of soup.

WATERCRESS SOUP WITH CHICKEN
Gai Sai Yong Choy Tong

4 oz. chicken stock
8 oz. uncooked chicken, diced
2 oz. onion diced
2 pieces celery cut in half lengthwise, then in 1/4" slices
8 oz. watercress

Bring stock, chicken, and vegetables (not the watercress) to a boil. Cover and cook 15 minutes at medium heat.
Add the watercress. Cover and cook 5 minutes. Check seasoning.

WATERCRESS SOUP WITH PORK
Sai Yong Choy Gee Yoke Tong

1/2 lb. lean pork, sliced thin in strips 1/2"x1"
4 cups water
1/2 lb. watercress washed and cut in 2" pieces
1/4 cup water
1 teaspoon soy sauce
1/8 teaspoon sesame oil

Bring pork and water to a boil. Let simmer, covered, for 10 minutes. Add the watercress. Cover and cook for 5 minutes. Add the 1/4 cup of water, soy sauce, and sesame oil. Stir.

HOT & SOUR SOUP
Suen Lat Tong

4 cups chicken stock
4 oz. uncooked chicken or lean pork cut in matchsticks
4 black mushrooms, soaked in warm water 30 minutes & cut
in 1/8" strips
6 pieces wood ears, soaked in warm water 30 minutes. Remove
any hard stems.
1/4 cup bamboo shoots, rinsed in cold water & cut in 1/8" strips
1 piece bean curd cut in 1/8" strips

Bring to a boil. Simmer for 10 minutes, covered. Add

1 tablespoon soy sauce
2 tablespoons wine vinegar
1/4 teaspoon pepper
2 tablespoons corn starch
1/4 cup water

Lower heat and stir until liquid becomes translucent, 1-2 minutes.
Slowly add

2 eggs well beaten
1/4 teaspoon sesame oil

Note: Wood ears and black mushrooms should be kept on hand
for dishes like this. A 2 oz. can of mushrooms may be substituted,
if you wish, but the flavor will not be the same.

VEGETARIAN SOUP

4 cups water
4 oz. onion minced fine
4 oz. carrots grated with coarse grater
4 oz. potato sliced thin
2 oz. celery cut in 1" pieces

Simmer, covered, 1 hour. Put through a sieve or run through a blender for 30 seconds. Return to pot. Bring again to a boil. Add

4 oz. canned mushrooms, stems and pieces
4 oz. water chestnuts sliced 1/8" thick

4 oz. bamboo shoots rinsed and cut in matchsticks
4 oz. Chinese celery or bok choy cut in slices 1/4" thick

Simmer 5 minutes. Add 1 tablespoon soy sauce. Stir.
A drop of peanut or sesame oil may be added to each bowl.

LEEK & MUSHROOM SOUP

On above recipe, increase the amount of mushrooms to 8 oz. Substitute in place of the water chestnuts and bamboo shoots, 8 oz. leeks cut in 1/2" pieces. Simmer 10-15 minutes.

QUICK VEGETARIAN SOUP

4 cups water
2 oz. onions miced fine
1 teaspoon dry sherry
2 tablespoons soy sauce

Bring to a boil. Simmer, covered, 10 minutes. Add

8 oz. canned mushrooms
4 oz. water chestnuts sliced 1/8" thick
4 oz. bamboo shoots rinsed and sliced 1/8"x1"x2"

Simmer for 5 minutes. Add

2 lettuce leaves cut in pieces 1"x2"
2 scallions cut in 1" pieces

Turn off heat. Stir 30 seconds. Serve.
Optional: To each bowl, add 1 drop sesame oil for strong flavor.
or 1 drop peanut oil for mild flavor.

CHINESE VEGETABLE SOUP
Choy Tong

4 cups stock
1/4 cup bamboo shoots, rinsed and cut in matchsticks
1/4 cup water chestnuts cut in slices 1/8" thick
4 black mushrooms, soaked in warm water 30 minutes, cut in 1/8" strips
8 snow peas or
2 oz. shredded lettuce
1 teaspoon soy sauce

Bring stock to a boil. Add bamboo shoots, water chestnuts, and black
mushrooms. Cover and simmer 10 minutes. Add the snow peas or
lettuce, along with the soy sauce. Cover and let stand 3 minutes.

BIRD'S NEST SOUP
In Wo Tong

2 oz. dried bird's nest. Soak overnight in cold water. Drain and rinse. Pick out any feathers.
1/2 teaspoon salt
1 slice ginger 1/4" thick
2 quarts water

Boil water, salt, and ginger. Add the bird's nest and simmer with cover for 1 hour. Remove ginger. Drain and discard the water. Store bird's nest until needed in a covered container in the refrigerator.

Place cooked bird's nest in a pot with
4 cups chicken stock
1/2 teaspoon salt
1 tablespoon dry sherry.

Boil. Then simmer with cover 1 hour. Add
2 oz. raw chicken meat minced fine, mixed with
2 egg whites.

Simmer 10 minutes. Add
2 tablespoons chicken stock
1 tablespoon corn starch.

Simmer and stir. Add
1 slice ham 1/8"x3"x3", cut in strips 1/4" wide
1 scallion minced fine.

Turn off heat and let stand undisturbed 5 minutes.
Nests of the best quality come from Borneo and Sumatra.
It is quite expensive, but very little is needed per portion.
It is nice to serve on special occasions, since it lets your company know how much you think of them.

Appetizers

Chinese appetizers come from all over the far east—Hawaii, Japan, India. Good food travels across borders easily. We learn of Marco Polo bringing pasta from the orient to Southern Europe: the same process of adoption goes on today. Cuisines, like language, like people, never stand still.

Any of these appetizers can be part of a large meal or served alone as a snack. Some definitions may help clear the way. Egg rolls are square noodles which have been filled with a vegetable mixture with meat or fish an optional addition. The noodles are folded (see diagram) and deep fat fried. They are served with any or all of these sauces—duck, hoisin, soy, or hot mustard. Spring rolls are round pancake or crepe dough filled with a similar mixture, folded (see diagram), and deep fat fried. They are served with the same sauces. Won tons are made with egg roll skins, generally filled with a meat mixture, folded (see diagram) and boiled with soup. Dumplings are neither a noodle, nor a pancake. They are close to our biscuit dough but usually do not contain any leavening. They are filled with a vegetable or fish mixture, folded, and cooked by steaming, boiling, or frying.

TEA EGGS

These are gorgeous. They look as though they are made of
marble or alabaster.

Take 6 or 12 eggs and cover with cold water. Bring to a slow
boil and let simmer for 15 minutes. Then put the pot in the
sink and run cold water into the pot until cool. Let stand 5
minutes. Remove eggs and gently crack the shell using the back
of a spoon, but do not remove the shells. Return eggs to pot and
add cold water to cover. Add

2 teaspoons salt
3 black tea bags
3 tablespoons soy sauce
1 whole star anise broken apart

Bring to a boil and then simmer 1 to 1-1/2 hours.
Cool and remove shell. These can be refrigerated for a few days.

EGG ROLL SKINS

2 cups sifted all purpose flour
1 egg
1/4 cup water

Mix until stiff. Cover with a damp cloth and let sit for 1/2 hour. Roll with a rolling pin or noodle making machine until the skin is a uniform 1/16" thick. If you are making egg rolls, cut in squares 7"x7". For won tons, cut in 3-1/2" squares, exactly one quarter of egg roll size. For filling and rolling won tons, see Soup Chapter or Index.

Dust lightly with flour before stacking or separate squares with wax paper so that the skins won't stick to each other. You can store these in your freezer for 6 months in a plastic bag. When you are ready, thaw them, and if they are too dry to be flexible, cover them with a damp towel. You can buy these skins frozen or fresh at a Chinese grocery store or some supermarkets.

To fill egg rolls, see diagram on facing page. Fillings are listed later in this chapter. Be careful to drain the fillings well before using—too much moisture will cause the rolls to blow apart in the frying. Seal the corner at the top with a bit of beaten egg Let the roll rest on this top corner until egg dries. Fry the rolls in a wok filled with peanut oil at 350-375 degrees until brown. Stand on end to drain and then place on a paper towel 1 minute.

You can freeze whatever you don't use immediately.
To reheat, bake 30 minutes in a 350 degree oven, if frozen
Or bake 15 minutes in a 350 degree oven, if thawed.

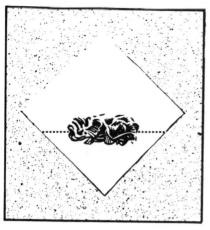

Step 1—Spoon 2 tablespoons drained filling on egg roll and fold upward on dotted line.

Step 2—Fold in opposite corners on dotted lines.

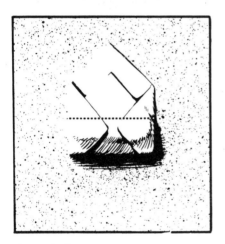

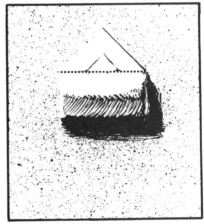

Step 3—Begin rolling upward on dotted line.

Step 4—Fold down top flap at dotted line and seal with a bit of beaten egg.

FOLDING THE EGG ROLL

SPRING ROLL WRAPPERS

1 cup sifted flour
1/4 teaspoon salt
1 egg
2 cups cold water

Mix together and let stand for 30 minutes to let air bubbles out.
Heat a heavy cast iron pan with 1/2 teaspoon peanut oil.
Pour in 2-3 tablespoons batter, tip the pan, and turn it until
batter spreads all over bottom of pan. Let set for 1-2 minutes.
Remove from pan and place on plate. Repeat until batter is used.
Be careful that pan is not too hot—the batter will harden as soon
as it hits the pan, before you have a chance to tilt it. Fry only
one side of the pancake, and when you fill these spring rolls,
place the filling on the fried side of the pancake. The unfried
side will then be exposed to the hot fat when you deep fry it.

To fill spring rolls, see diagram on facing page. Fillings are listed
later in this chapter. Be careful to drain the filling well before
using—too much moisture will cause the rolls to blow apart in
frying. Seal the top flap with a mixture of 1 tablespoon flour
and 2 tablespoons cold water. Let the finished roll rest on this
flap for 30 minutes until mixture dries. Fry the rolls in 2-3"
of peanut oil in a wok at 350-375 degrees until they are brown.
About 6-8 minutes should do the job.

You can freeze whatever you do not use immediately. To reheat,
bake in 350 degree oven 30 minutes if frosted, 15 minutes if
thawed.

Spring rolls are easier to make from scratch than egg rolls, but
are not quite so crisp when fried.

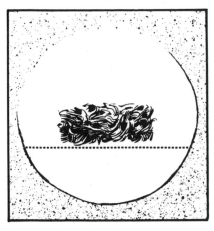

Step 1—Place 2 tablespoons drained filling on spring roll. Fold upward on dotted line.

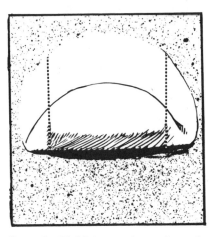

Step 2—Fold inwards at dotted line.

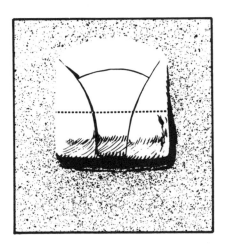

Step 3—Begin rolling upward at dotted line.

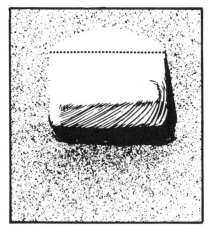

Step 4—Fold down top at dotted line and seal with flour paste.

FOLDING THE SPRING ROLL

CHICKEN FILLING FOR EGG ROLLS OR SPRING ROLLS

Plate 1

8 oz. boned chicken breast cut 1/8"x1/8"x2" pieces. Firm in freezer before slicing.

4 oz. canned mushrooms, stems and pieces

Plate 2

6 oz. shredded cabbage

4 oz. bamboo shoots, rinsed and shredded

2 oz. water chestnuts shredded

6 oz. bean sprouts

Cup 1

1 teaspoon soy sauce

1 teaspoon dry sherry

1 teaspoon sugar

Wok or pan, medium heat

1 tablespoon peanut oil

1/2 teaspoon salt

1 clove garlic minced fine

When garlic starts to turn golden, add plate 1 and stir until chicken turns white.

Add plate 2 and stir 3 minutes.

Add cup 1 and cover 2 minutes.

Turn fire off and place in colander to drain. Place a small plate on top of mixture and put a weight on top of the plate.

Spring
Rolls

PORK & SHRIMP FILLING FOR EGG OR SPRING ROLLS

Plate 1
1/2 lb ground raw pork.

Plate 2
1./2 lb. raw cleaned shrimp cut in pieces the size of peas

Plate 3
2 cups cabbage shredded
4 oz. bamboo shoots rinsed and cut in matchsticks
4 oz. water chestnuts cut in matchsticks
2 teaspoon soy sauce
1 teaspoon salt
1 teaspoon sugar

Wok or pan, medium heat
1 tablespoon peanut oil

Add plate 1 and stir until all red is gone, 4 minutes.
Add plate 2 and stir fry 2 minutes.
Add plate 3, stir 1 minute, and simmer, covered, 5 minutes.
Add 2 scallions minced fine and place mixture in colander
with a weighted plate on top. When drained, proceed to
fill rolls per previous diagrams.

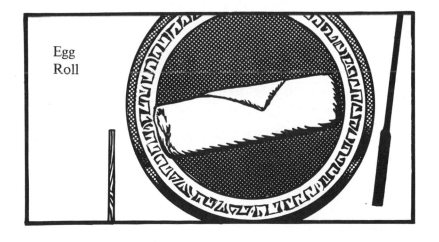

Egg
Roll

VEGETABLE FILLING FOR EGG OR SPRING ROLLS

Plate 1
6 black mushrooms, soaked in warm water 30 minutes, drained and cut in strips 1/8" wide

Plate 2
2 stalks celery cut in 2" pieces, then shredded lengthwise
1 green pepper in strips 1/8"x2" long
2 oz. bamboo shoots 1/8"x1/8"x2"

Plate 3
6 oz. cabbage 1/8"x2". You can use 1/2 green cabbage, 1/2 red.
4 oz. bean sprouts
4 water chestnuts cut in 1/8" slices then 1/8" strips
2 scallions cut 2" long, then shredded lengthwise

Cup 1
2 teaspoons soy sauce
1 teaspoon sugar

Wok or pan, medium heat
1 tablespoon peanut oil
1/2 teaspoon salt
2 cloves garlic minced fine

When garlic is golden, add plate 1 and stir 3 minutes.
Add plate 2 and stir 3 minutes.
Add plate 3 and stir 1 minute.
Add cup 1 and stir 1 minute Cover and turn off heat. Let stand a few minutes. Then pour into colander to drain off excess fluid. A weighted small plate will help.

STEAK STRIPS
Shu Ngow Yoke

Take 8 oz. flank steak and firm it in freezer. Slice 1/4" across the flank—pieces should be 6"-10" long depending on the piece they are cut from. You may also cut pieces from a round steak 3/4" thick. Place the flank or steak pieces in the following marinade:

1/4 cup soy sauce
1 clove garlic minced fine
1 tablespoon dry sherry
1 slice ginger 1/8" thick, minced fine
1/4 cup chicken stock
1 teaspoon brown sugar
1 teaspoon peanut oil

Marinate in the refrigerator for at least 3 hours, but no more than 12 hours.

Weave on skewers, bamboo or metal. Soak bamboo skewers in water first. Broil 3"-4" from coals until done.

SPICED CHICKEN BONES

This delicacy is usually saved for the chef in restaurants. You may want to munch on them as you proceed with other recipes.

Take the chicken bones which have been used for stock. Heat 1 tablespoon peanut oil in a wok, add 1/2 teaspoon salt, and 1 clove garlic minced fine. Add the chicken bones and stir fry 10 minutes. Add

1 tablespoon sherry
1 tablespoon soy sauce
1 tablespoon catsup
2 teaspoons Worcestershire sauce

Stir fry 3 minutes and serve.

DUMPLINGS

Some translate dumplings as Dot Hearts. Whatever you call them, once you have tried them, you will be hooked for life. When I was young, only a few restaurants served them. Now there are many more restaurants, serving 50-100 different varieties of dumplings.

When you go to a Dim Sum House, a waiter will come around with a tray on which are plates with assortments of dumplings. You point to the plate you want. At the end of the meal, the number of plates you have consumed are tallied for your bill. It is best to go with a few friends—that way you can share in many varieties of Dim Sums.

Wrappers
2 cups flour
1 cup hot water
Mix until uniform, knead, then cover and let stand 30 minutes. Roll into a rope 1" in diameter. Cut in pieces 1" thick. On a lightly floured board, press these into cakes. Then roll out until they are 3" in diameter and about 1/8" thick.

Filling
1 lb. lean ground pork
4 scallions minced fine
2 water chestnuts minced fine
1 slice 1/8" thick ginger, minced fine
1 oz. bamboo shoots rinsed and minced fine
1 teaspoon sesame oil
1 tablespoon soy sauce
1 tablespoon dry sherry
3 black mushrooms soaked in warm water 30 minutes, cut in pea size pieces

Blend the above ingredients.

Forming
Place 2 teaspoons of filling on each wrapper. Fold wrapper in
half and pinch at center and both ends. Don't let any filling
get in the way Form 3 pleats on each side of the center on one
side only. This will cause the dumpling to form a crescent when
viewed from the top. See diagram

Steaming
Place a damp cloth on the tray of the steamer. Fill the tray with
dumplings, but do not let them touch each other. Steam for
about 20 minutes.

Boiling
Drop in 8 quarts of boiling water. Boil gently for 10 minutes.

Frying
Place 2 tablespoons peanut oil in a bottom of a large flat pan.
When the oil begins to smoke, put the dumplings in with the
pleats up, sides just touching each other. After bottoms brown,
2-4 minutes, add 1 cup water or stock and cover pan. Steam in
pan for 8-10 minutes.

Sauces
Serve with soy sauce mixed with vinegar (red Chinese) or hot
mustard and hoisin sauce.

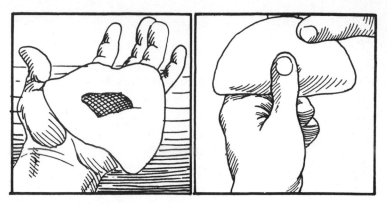

Place 2 teaspoons filling on each wrapper Fold in half.

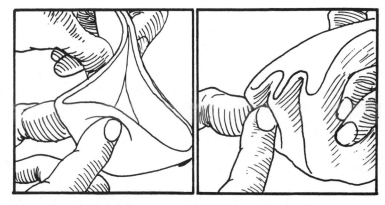

Pinch at center and both ends. Form 3 pleats on each side.

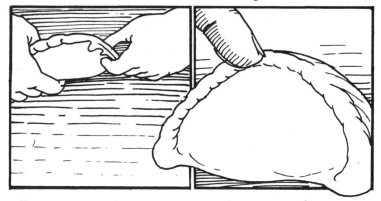

The dumpling forms a crescent when viewed from top.

FORMING DUMPLINGS, Recipe page 61

STEAMED DUMPLINGS

Wrappers
2 cups flour
1 cup boiling water
1/8 teaspoon salt
Mix until dough is uniform. Cover for 15 minutes. Then roll out
in a rope 1" in diameter. Cut pieces 1" long and roll out until
3" in diameter. Fill with 2 heaping teaspoons filling in center.
Then form wrapper up around filling like a tulip. Press finished
dumpling on table to flatten the bottom.

Or use egg roll skins bought in store. Bring sides up as in
drawing, to make the dumpling resemble a tulip. You may have
to cover the skins with a damp cloth to keep them from drying
out.

Filling
1 lb. lean ground pork
4 oz. raw shrimp minced the size of peas
2 scallions, white part, minced fine
3 black mushrooms, soaked in warm water 30 minutes, then cut
in pieces 1/4"x1/4"
1/2 teaspoon sesame oil, optional
1/2 teaspoon salt
1/2 teaspoon sugar
1 tablespoon corn starch
2 teaspoons soy sauce
1 tablespoon dry sherry

Mix well. Then put 2 teaspoons filling in center and fold like
a tulip.

Steaming
Wipe plate with peanut oil and set the dumplings on the plate.
They should not touch each other. Place in steamer 15-20
minutes. Serve with hot mustard or hoisin sauce or duck sauce.
These can be made ahead of time. Cover the plate with foil
and refrigerate until needed.
This recipe will yield 30 or more dumplings.

SHRIMP TOAST
Har Do See

8-10 oz. shrimp. Remove shell and devein. Then mince fine.
1 teaspoon soy sauce
1 egg well beaten
4 water chestnuts minced
1 tablespoon corn starch
Mix in a mixing bowl until uniform.

Cut 8 slices of day old white bread or lightly toasted fresh bread in diagonal slices. Remove crusts first.

Divide shrimp mixture equally among the bread slices. Spread with a butter spreader and press down to make sure mix adheres to bread. Sprinkle sesame seeds on each piece and press into mix.

Heat 2-3 cups peanut oil in wok to 350 degrees and lower each piece of bread shrimp side down into the oil with a slotted spatula. Fry 3 minutes. Turn over and fry other side 1 minute. Remove and drain on a paper towel. Then keep warm in oven or heated tray.

Your friends will want this recipe—it is delicious and very easy to make.

SHRIMP BALLS
Har Kow

1 lb. shrimp. Shell and remove vein. Mince fine.
6 water chestnuts minced fine
1 scallion, white part only, minced fine
1 slice ginger 1/8" thick, minced fine
2 black mushrooms soaked in warm water and minced fine
or 1/2 oz. canned mushrooms minced fine
1/2 teaspoon salt
1 egg
1 teaspoon corn starch.

Mix well. Then form into balls, using 1 heaping teaspoon as
a measure for each one. Deep fry in peanut oil at 375 degrees
until light golden in color. Drain well.

Before frying, you can dip the balls in a batter of
1 beaten egg
1/4 cup corn starch
1/2 cup flour
1 teaspoon baking powder
Add enough water to make a smooth batter.

Use chopsticks to roll shrimp balls in batter. Lift out and fry.
Hoisin, duck sauce, and hot mustard are the usual condiments
for this dish in tea houses. They can be made ahead of time
and kept warm in the oven.

CRISPY CHICKEN WINGS

When I worked in a metal shop in Binghamton, I used a welding torch and cooked in the shop for the people who worked there. This dish was the all time favorite.

Wash and pat dry 3 lbs. chicken wings. They cook fast—they aren't as thick as drumsticks. The best size to buy is 4-6 wings to the lb. Cut the tip off the wings and save for soup.

Mix in a large bowl:

1/4 cup dry sherry
1/4 cup soy sauce—Kikkoman works best for this recipe
1/2 cup corn starch

Use a heavy spoon made of metal or wood, since the mixture will be quite heavy. Dip the wings, 1 lb. at a time, into the soy sauce mixture and toss them about so that they are coated. Lift out with tongs and drop into 375 degree peanut oil. Use a thermometer to make sure the temperature is maintained. While one batch is frying, place the second batch in the batter. When they are done (they will be very dark because of the soy sauce in the batter), drain in a wire basket and then on paper towels. They can be kept warm in a 250 degree oven.

Strain oil when it has cooled off to get rid of any particles. While you are doing the cooking, a Japanese oil skimmer is handy to remove particles from the bottom of the wok.

RUMAKI

4 oz. fresh chicken livers
1 cup water
1/4 teaspoon 5 spice, optional
1 teaspoon soy sauce

Bring to a boil in a wok and simmer 5 minutes.
Place in freezer to firm. Then slice diagonally 1/4" thick.
Drain a small can of water chestnuts and wrap a piece of liver
around the chestnut. It should overlap about 1/4".

Wrap a piece of uncooked bacon around the liver. Let it overlap
about 1/4". Push a toothpick through the piece,from one side to
the other. The water chestnut should be visible from two sides.
Roll in brown sugar. Place in tray in oven at 425 degrees for 15
minutes or until bacon is light brown. This can be held on a steam
table or warm tray or warm oven until needed.

HAWAIIAN PLATTER

You can put together a platter of hot tasty appetizers from this chapter as well as from other chapters—Barbequed Spareribs and Barbequed Chicken Wings, Roast Pork, Egg Rolls, Shrimp Toast, and so on. When your guests are finished eating, they may appreciate a hot damp towel. You can prepare these by dipping one corner of a clean small towel in hot water mixed with lemon juice (to cut the grease on hands) and rolling up the towel with the wet portion inside. Keep these warm in a steamer. Or you can buy commercial towels packed in aluminum foil envelopes.

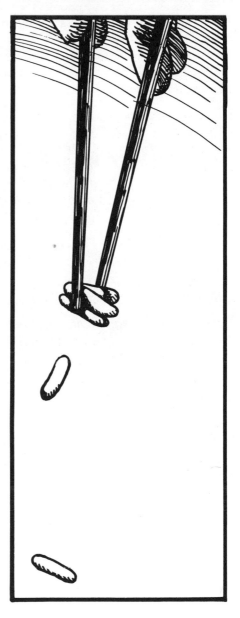

Rice

Many Americans complain after eating in a Chinese restaurant they are hungry one hour later. Chinese make the same complaint after eating in an American restaurant. The answer is simple. Americans don't eat as much rice as the Chinese do, and the Chinese do not eat as much bread.

Think back to the last time you went to a restaurant in Chinatown. You looked at the big bowl of rice on the table and wondered, "Do they really expect me to eat all this?" Chinese people eat a great deal of rice. For instance, one dish of Moo Goo Gai Pan which will feed one American will feed four Chinese because a lot of rice is downed with the chicken. It is a very economical way of eating.

There are two kinds of rice: brown (unprocessed) and white (processed). The Chinese generally use white rice. You can substitute brown rice—it will give a different flavor and texture to any dish but is very nutritious.

Rice, brown or white, comes in long grain and short grain. Long grain rice is superior for boiled, steamed, or fried dishes. The grains, when properly cooked, remain separate, not sticky. Short grain rice can be used for jook where the stickiness is desirable.

BOILED WHITE RICE
Chinese Rule of Thumb Method

3 cups water
1 cup washed white rice

Use long grain white rice. Wash in cold water, rubbing with hands to remove starch. Rinse repeatedly in cold water until water is clear.

Place drained rice in heavy pot. Level off the rice with the palm of your hand. Slowly pour enough water into the pot so that when you place your thumb down on top of the rice, the water will come up to the joint. This should be about 3 cups, depending on the size of the pot used. Bring to a boil, reduce heat, and cover with tight fitting lid (not a vapor seal type). Let remain for 30 minutes.

Do not stir or lift the cover for any reason for at least 30 minutes. The rice can be left a maximum of 60 minutes if necessary. If it starts to dry out, add 1/4 cup of water to the pot and continue cooking at a simmer, covered.

If the pot is attractive, use it as a serving dish. With its cover on, it will stay warm during the meal. Refrigerate any leftover rice.

BOILED BROWN RICE

3 cups cold water
1 cup washed brown rice

Basically same method as above. Use a heavy pot. Bring to a boil. Cover and simmer for 60-90 minutes. Refrigerate any leftover rice.

VARIATIONS ON RULE OF THUMB RICE
Slow Boat Rice

3 cups water
1 cup washed white rice

Follow Rule of Thumb Method on preceding page. Instead of bringing the pot to a boil and then using a cover, cover the pot first and cook at lowest possible heat for 45 minutes to 1 hour and 15 minutes. You will have to check to see when the rice is done. On my stove at the lowest setting, it takes exactly one hour.

If your stove cannot operate at very low heat, buy a 6" wide, 1/2" high metal disk at your hardware store. It is made of two circles of sheet metal separated by an air space which will cut direct heat transfer from your stove to the pan and therefore lower the heat.

Volcano Rice

Use same proportion of rice to water as above.
Put pot on medium heat uncovered until the water above the rice boils away and small 1/4" holes appear on the surface of the rice.
Cover pot and simmer 20-30 minutes.

Double Boiler Rice

Prepare top of boiler with rice and water as above.
Put enough water in bottom of boiler so that it doesn't boil away. Place top of boiler over medium heat and bottom of boiler over high heat. When both pots boil, lower heat on bottom of boiler so that it boils gently. Place top pot on bottom pot and cover. Rice will be done in 45-60 minutes without the slightest worry of burning. When done, the top lid can be left ajar and the heat lowered. The rice will be ready to serve for quite a while.

FAST RICE SINGAPORE STYLE

1 quart water
1 cup washed rice

When I am in a hurry or have a few other dishes to watch, I use this method. It is the easiest way to prepare white rice.
Bring water to a boil. Add the rice.

When the water boils again, reduce heat to low and continue cooking without a cover. The rice should continue boiling but at a low level. It should be done in 15 minutes.
Pour into a colander and pour 2 cups cold water over the rice. Stir with a chopstick. Rice can be served immediately.

RICE STEAMED IN OVEN

2 cups water
1 cup washed rice

When the oven is in use, you can save electricity by making rice at the same time. Place rice (white) in a casserole. Add the water. You can double or triple the proportions if you like. Cover tightly and place in 325-350 degree oven for about 30 minutes. If you use a pyrex clear glass dish, you can check on the rice easily while it is cooking.

RICE STEAMED IN STEAMER

Use the same proportion of ingredients as above. A Chinese steamer can be used with more than one tray in simultaneous use. Steam rice in the lowest tray and use the upper trays for items requiring more attention.

Place rice in colander in tray. Cover and steam 45-60 minutes. The colander will prevent the rice from becoming soggy—any moisture that drips from the top will drain through the bottom holes. But make sure that the colander is large enough for the rice to expand. Each cup of washed white rice will expand to 3 cups of steamed rice.

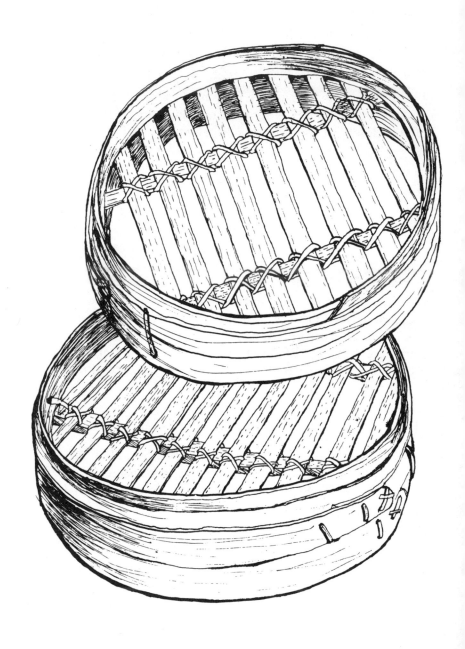

CHINESE BAMBOO STEAMER

HOW TO STORE & REHEAT LEFTOVER RICE

Place any leftover rice in refrigerator overnight uncovered. Cover the rice tightly the next morning. Rice stored this way at 40 degrees in the refrigerator can last up to a week. I usually make enough rice so that I have sufficient left over to last about four days.

There are many ways to reheat the rice.

In A Heavy Pot
Place 1 cup leftover cold rice in a heavy pot. Add 1/4-1/2 teaspoon water and simmer, covered. The rice should steam itself to serving temperature in about 10 minutes.

In A Colander (Aluminum or Stainless Steel)
Place 1 cup leftover cold rice in a colander and cover. Place over a pot which contains enough water so that it won't boil away. Steam rice 5 minutes. The rice can be left in the colander over the pot if it is not needed immediately.

In A Double Boiler
Transfer the rice (1 cup) to the top part of a double boiler. Bring water in the bottom part of the double boiler to a boil, reduce heat, and place the top part on top of the bottom part. Make sure the lid on the top part is slightly ajar. Boil for 15 minutes until rice reaches serving temperature.

In Any Pot
Bring 1 quart of water to a boil, add 1 cup leftover cold rice. Stir to break up any lumps and cook for 1-2 minutes. Then strain through a colander.

BOILED RICE WITH ADDITIONAL INGREDIENTS

Chinese cooks don't waste anything. As long as rice is steaming in a pot, additional ingredients can be placed on top of the rice and cooked at the same time.

Prepare Rule of Thumb Rice. When pot starts to boil, reduce heat to simmer, cover, and cook 5 minutes. Set the timer to make sure you will be accurate.
After 5 minutes have passed, add whatever ingredients you like, recover and simmer an additional 25 minutes.

LOP CHUNG & RICE

When the rice has cooked 5 minutes, add 2 links of Lop Chung (Chinese sausage), about 4 oz., rinsed and sliced diagonally in 1/4" thickness.
Proceed with preparation as above.

CHICKEN & LOP CHUNG ON RICE

Small mixing bowl
4 dried black mushrooms soaked in warm water 30 minutes, cut in 1/4" strips
6 oz. boned raw chicken in 1/4"x1" pieces
1 tablespoon soy sauce
1 tablespoon dry sherry
Marinate for at least 30 minutes.

Plate 1
2 links Lop Chung, about 4 oz., rinsed & sliced diagonally in 1/4" thickness

Plate 2
2 scallions, white & green parts, cut in 1/4" slices

Add contents of mixing bowl and plate 1 to rice after 5 minute period has passed. Cook 25 minutes. Turn heat off. Add plate 2. Cover once more, and let stand at least 3 minutes.

FRIED RICE WITH VARIATIONS
Chow Fan

Plate 1
2 cups leftover rice, 1 day old if possible
2 oz. onion minced coarsely

Plate 2
1 egg scrambled—Heat 1/2 teaspoon oil in wok, add egg. Cook &
stir until broken into pieces.

Plate 3
1-2 scallions, white part only, cut in 1/4" pieces

Wok or pan, medium heat
2 tablespoons peanut oil
1/4 teaspoon salt
1 clove garlic minced fine

Add plate 1 and cook 5 minutes. Stir and press out lumps in rice.
Add plate 2. Stir 2 minutes
Add 1/2 teaspoon molasses. Stir until rice has brown coating.
Add plate 3 and stir 1 minute.

SHRIMP FRIED RICE
Har Chow Fan

Boil shrimp 3 minutes, drain, and add to plate 2.

CHICKEN FRIED RICE
Gai Chow Fan

Cut raw boned chicken in 1/4" to 1/2" pieces.
Cook in 1/2 teaspoon oil 4 minutes. Add to plate 2

ROAST PORK FRIED RICE
Char Shu Chow Fan

Use leftover roast pork. Cut in 1/2" pieces. Add to plate 2.

LOBSTER FRIED RICE
Lung Har Chow Fan

Boil lobster 7 minutes. When cool, remove lobster meat from
shell. Cut in 1/2" pieces. Add to plate 2.

JOOK OR CONGEE

1 cup white rice washed until liquid is clear
2-1/2 quarts water

Bring to a boil. Then lower heat. Keep cover slightly ajar while cooking. Time: 1-1/2 to 2 hours. Please note that no seasoning is in the basic stock. When ready the soup will be thick with a slight layer of water on top. More water can be added for proper consistency if needed.

When ready to serve, place in each bowl
1 lettuce leaf cut in 1/4" strips
1" scallion cut in 1/4" pieces
1 tablespoon any cooked meat cut in 1/4" strips
1 teaspoon soy sauce

Add the cooked jook and stir. Let stand at least 2 minutes.

Serve jook by itself or as a soup to go with a meal.

Restaurants catering to Westerners do not serve this dish. Nevertheless, it is exceedingly good and you should try it—it is handy—it can be kept ready in back of the stove so that you can make an impromptu meal in a hurry. It is flexible—you can vary it with leftovers for different dishes.And it is extremely cheap— 1 cup of raw rice makes 2 quarts of jook.

My favorite time to go into a Chinese restaurant is when it is closed, and I can visit with the chef and have a bowl of jook. What does it taste like? Like rice, but with an improved flavor from the long cooking. The best jook I ever tasted had assorted vegetables and tangerine peel cooked with it.

Variation—Before the jook is cooked, add a few chicken hearts cleaned and split, a few chicken gizzards cleaned and cut in half, and some pork bones with all the fat removed.

Noodles

Noodles are made from flour and water, with eggs sometimes added. The flour may come from wheat, rice, or beans (mung or soy). In this country, wheat and rice noodles can be purchased fresh or dried, whereas bean noodles are available only in dry form. Fresh noodles taste much better, but dried noodles have a longer life on the shelf.

You cook wheat noodles the same way you cook ordinary noodles. Rice noodles or rice sticks (Sha Ho Fun) are boiled 5-10 minutes depending on the brand. They come in 2" coils, about 1/16" thick x 1/4" wide. Bean noodles or cellophane noodles or long rice are boiled in a few minutes—watch out that you don't overcook them—they quickly turn to mush.

You are familiar with the taste of wheat noodles. Rice noodles taste like rice pudding, a bit sweeter than wheat noodles. The two can be used interchangeably in most dishes.

Bean noodles have no flavor at all. They absorb surrounding flavors totally. The texture of the bean noodles is also different. They are decidedly slippery.

FRIED NOODLES

Fried noodles are served with soup in most Chinese restaurants. After the soup is finished, the noodles are usually left on the table, and it becomes a finger food while waiting for other dishes to arrive. Fried noodles are also used as a base for Chow Mein. The noodles are placed in a 1/4" layer on the serving platter with the meat and vegetable mixture on top. The noodles absorb the moisture from the gravy and enhance the flavor.

Method 1

When you buy wrappers for egg rolls or won tons, you may find some which are not suitable—too thin in spots or too dry to roll. Cut these wrappers in 1/4" strips and deep fat fry them at 350 degrees F. until they are light brown. Drain on paper towels. Serve or store in airtight containers.

Method 2

2 quarts water
1 tablespoon salt
4-6 oz. egg noodles, about 1/8" to 1/4" wide.

Boil 8-10 minutes. Drain in colander. Rinse with cold water to stop cooking process and to get rid of surface starch. Spread out on tray to dry. When noodles are dry to the touch, deep fry them until light brown at 350 degrees. Drain on paper towels. Serve or store in an airtight container.

Method 3

8 oz. sifted all purpose flour
2 eggs
1/8 teaspoon salt
1 teaspoon peanut oil

Mix with chopsticks. Then add a little water to make a smooth dough. The amount of water needed will depend on the type or brand of flour you use. When the dough is smooth, knead with your hands for a few minutes. Then cover and refrigerate for 15 minutes.

Roll out on a floured board. Using a pizza roller, cut the dough in strips as wide as you wish. Or use a parsley cutter which can cut up to 10 strips at a time. Let these strips dry for 30 minutes. Deep fry them at 350 degrees until light brown. Drain on paper towels. Serve or store in an airtight container.

NOODLE TRICKS

Noodle Nests
Look in a French cooking supply store for a pair of strainers used to form noodles into nests. Or obtain a 4-5" diameter strainer with a flat bottom. Line the bottom and sides with 2-3 oz. of cooked noodles. Heat oil to 350 degrees and lower the strainer into the oil for 5-10 seconds until the noodles are set in shape. Turn the strainer over and let the noodles slip back into the oil. Fry until golden brown in color. Remove and drain on paper towel. Chop Suey or any dish with a thick gravy can be placed on this nest. It is a nice touch to surround the nest with a circle of cooked white rice.

Noodle Pancakes
Cooked noodles can be formed into a cake about 4-5" diameter and then deep fried until golden. This pancake can be served on top of any dish with thick gravy. Or use small pancakes in soup.

Pan Fried Noodles
After you cook noodles by Method 3, let them dry to the touch. Place in a bowl and add 2 tablespoons peanut oil. Toss to coat the noodles until most of the oil is absorbed. Place on rack in steamer and steam for 10-15 minutes. Remove and let cool and get dry to the touch. Place about 4 tablespoons peanut oil in a flat frying pan about 10" diameter. Slowly brown the noodles on one side and then slowly brown the other side. The noodles will not puff up as they do in the deep fry method, nor will they be as crispy. It sometimes is more convenient to cook them this way. They will also not absorb as much gravy as the crisp noodles.

CHICKEN LO MEIN
Gai Lo Mein

Plate 1
4 oz. raw boned chicken, sliced in strips 1/4"x1/4"x2" long

Plate 2
4 oz. dried noodles
1 tablespoon peanut oil
2 oz. waterchestnuts cut in 1/4" slices
2 oz. bamboo shoots cut 1/4"x1/4"x2" long, rinsed in cold water
and parboiled for 3 minutes
2 oz. celery 1/4"x2" long
Boil the noodles for 10 minutes. Drain, rinse with cold water,
and drain again. Spread out on a platter. After they are dry to the
touch, mix with 1 tablespoon peanut oil until the noodles are
coated.

Cup 1
1 teaspoon dry sherry
1 teaspoon sugar
1/8 teaspoon sesame oil
3 tablespoons oyster sauce
1 teaspoon soy sauce

Wok or pan, medium heat
1 tablespoon peanut oil
1/4 teaspoon salt
1 clove garlic minced fine
1 scallion minced fine

When garlic is golden, add plate 1 and stir until chicken starts to
brown (4-5 minutes).
Add plate 2 and stir 4 minutes.
Add cup 1 and stir 2 minutes.

Variation—You can use raw pork or shrimp on plate 1 in place
of the chicken.

CELLOPHANE NOODLES WITH PORK & SHRIMP
Chow Foon Shee

Plate 1
8 oz. lean pork cut in 1/8" slices, then in 1/8" pieces 2" long
4 oz. canned mushrooms cut in 1/8" slices

Plate 2
8 oz. shrimp. Remove shell and devein.
4 oz. package cellophane noodles. Soak in warm water 20 minutes.
Then cut in 2" pieces

Plate 3
1 egg scrambled then fried in 1 tablespoon oil in wok.
Rotate wok until egg is thin and fried. Roll egg up like jelly roll
and cut in 1/4" strips. Then cut in half.
1 scallion cut in 1/4" pieces

Cup 1
1/2 cup chicken stock
1 tablespoon soy sauce
1 tablespoon dry sherry

Wok or pan, medium heat
2 tablespoons peanut oil
1/2 teaspoon salt
1 clove garlic minced fine

When garlic is golden, add plate 1 and stir 5 minutes until pork
is brown.
Add plate 2 and stir 2 minutes.
Add cup 1 and cover for 5 minutes until gravy is absorbed.
Add plate 3 and stir 1 minute.

More vegetables can easily be added to plate 2 for variety or
to enlarge the dish. Half a cup of mixed vegetables (green
peppers, bamboo shoots, water chestnuts, celery, etc.) can be
used in 1/8"x1/8"x2" pieces.

CHICKEN YEE FU MEIN

Plate 1
4 oz raw boned chicken cut in cubes 1/2"
4 pieces dried black mushrooms with stems broken off

Plate 2
Noodles in a single package
1 scallion cut in 1/4" pieces
6 snow peas. Remove string but leave whole.

Heat 2-1/4 cups water to boiling.
Add plate 1 and simmer 20 minutes.
Add plate 2 and simmer 3 minutes.
Add powder from noodle package.
If you wish to have the scallions crisper, add them when you
add the powder.

QUICK CHICKEN YEE FU MEIN

Plate 1
4 oz. chicken, cooked, sliced thin
1 oz. onion sliced in tangerine wedges
2 oz. canned mushrooms sliced thin
1 stalk celery sliced thin
1 package noodles

Heat 2 cups water to boiling.
Add plate 1 and simmer 3 minutes. Add powder from package.

Note:
Although Yee Fu Mein is a Japanese noodle, many Chinese use
it for home cooking, and many Chinese restaurants use it for
special dishes. It is good for a quick dish since it can be finished
4 minutes after you boil some water. It can also be made into
an elaborate dish.

When you open the package, remove the envelope containing the
soup stock base, and add it at the last stage of cooking.

STIR FRIED YEE FU MEIN WITH HAM
Chow Yee Fu Mein

Plate 1

4 oz. ham sliced 1/4"x1/2"x1"

4 black mushrooms soaked in warm water 30 minutes, cut in 1/4" strips
2 oz. onion cut in tangerine wedges
4 water chestnuts cut in slices 1/4" thick
1 oz. bamboo shoots cut in 1/4"x1/2x1" slices

Plate 2

4 oz. bean sprouts
Noodles in a single package cooked according to package directions

Cup 1

1/4 cup stock
1 tablespoon soy sauce
1 tablespoon oyster sauce, optional

Wok or pan, medium heat

1 tablespoon peanut oil
1/2 teaspoon salt
1 clove garlic minced fine

When garlic turns golden, add plate 1 and stir 3 minutes.
Add plate 2 and stir 3 minutes.
Add cup 1 and stir 2-3 minutes until noodles have a dark coat and most of the liquid is absorbed. If you let the noodles dry a bit (on plate 2) before adding them to the wok, they will absorb the flavor of the sauce faster. Do not use the soup base envelope from the package in this recipe. Save for other uses.

Vegetables

These dishes are not only suitable for vegetarians but are also good side dishes to help lower food costs. They are very quick to make, with a minimum of preparation.

You will need a vegetable stock, but regular chicken stock can be used. The two are interchangeable. You can make vegetable stock easily by dissolving 1 bouillon cube in 1 cup of water. The mixture can be kept in a bottle in the refrigerator for instant use. Better stock can be made by using 1 cup of cut up vegetables in 1 quart of water. Bring to a boil, cover, and simmer until the vegetables are done. Strain and pour back 1/2 cup of hot stock over the vegetables. You can use this as a vegetable soup. Refrigerate the remainder.

Vegetarians should consult the index for various egg dishes to help round out their menus.

STIR FRIED FRESH ASPARAGUS
Gna Shun

Plate 1
Cut bottom third of 1 lb. asparagus in 1" diagonal slices.
Discard white and green inedible portion.

Plate 2
Cut tips of asparagus. Cut remainder of stalks in 1" diagonal slices.

Cup 1
1 tablespoon soy sauce
1 tablespoon dry sherry

Wok or pan, medium heat
1 tablespoon peanut oil
1/2 teaspoon salt
1 clove garlic minced fine

When garlic starts to turn golden, add plate 1 and stir 3 minutes.
Add plate 2 and stir 1 minute.
Add cup 1 and stir 1 minute.

STIR FRIED STRING BEANS
Chow Dow Jay

Plate 1
1 lb. fresh string beans. Remove stems, cut diagonally in 2" pieces.

Cup 1
1/2 cup stock

Wok or pan, medium heat
2 tablespoons peanut oil
1 teaspoon salt

Cook 20 seconds.
Add plate 1 and stir 2 minutes.
Add cup 1, simmer covered 5 minutes.
Remove cover, stir, and serve.

BAMBOO SHOOTS WITH BLACK MUSHROOMS
Jook Sun Dong Goo

Plate 1
8 oz. bamboo shoots, drained & rinsed in cold water, then cut in slices 1/4"x1"x2"

Cup 1
1/2 cup stock
1 tablespoon corn starch

Wok or pan
1/2 cup stock
4 black mushrooms rinsed, then cut in 4 parts, stem removed
1 tablespoon soy sauce
1 tablespoon dry sherry

Heat mixture in wok to a boil, then simmer covered 10 minutes. You should still have a little liquid left.

Add 1 tablespoon peanut oil. Stir 1 minute over medium heat.

Add plate 1. Stir 2 minutes over medium heat.

Add cup 1. Stir until gravy starts to thicken.

BAMBOO SHOOTS WITH CANNED MUSHROOMS
Jook Sun Moo Goo

Plate 1
8 oz. bamboo shoots, drained & rinsed in cold water, then cut in slices 1/8"x1"x2"

Plate 2
8 oz. canned mushrooms, stems & pieces, sliced in 1/8" bits

Cup 1
2 tablespoons soy sauce
1 tablespoon dry sherry
1 teaspoon sugar

Wok or pan, medium heat
2 tablespoons peanut oil
1/2 teaspoon salt

Add plate 1 and stir 2 minutes.
Add plate 2 and stir 2 minutes.
Add cup 1 and cover 2 minutes.

If you wish a gravy, add 1/4 cup stock and 1 tablespoon corn starch. Cook and stir, until gravy thickens.

STIR FRIED BROCCOLI
Chow Gai Lon Choy

Plate 1
Discard hard bottom of broccoli. Cut stems in 1" pieces.
Stems over 1" thick cut in half.

Plate 2
Cut flowers in 1" pieces.

Cup 1
1/2 cup stock
1/2 teaspoon sugar

Wok or pan, medium heat
2 tablespoons peanut oil
1 teaspoon salt

After 20 seconds, add plate 1 and stir 2 minutes.
Add plate 2 and stir 1 minute.
Add cup 1. Cover and cook for 5 minutes. Liquid should be
almost gone.

STIR FRIED CELERY
Chow Gun Choy

Plate 1
1 cup celery cut in 1" diagonal slices. If you use the outside stalks,
use the top 2/3 and save the rest for soup stock.

Cup 1
1/4 cup stock
1 teaspoon sherry
1 teaspoon soy sauce

Wok or pan, medium heat
1 tablespoon peanut oil
1/2 teaspoon salt
1 clove garlic minced fine
1 slice 1/8" thick ginger root minced fine

When garlic is golden, add plate 1 and stir 2 minutes.
Add cup 1 and stir, then turn heat up to high and stir 2-3 minutes
more until most of liquid is gone.

STIR FRIED BEAN CURD
Chow Tau Fu

Plate 1
3 cakes fresh bean curd cut in 1" squares. Fresh bean curd is sold
in 3"x3" squares.

Cup 1
1-1/2 tablespoons soy sauce
1/2 cup stock
1/2 teaspoon sugar

Wok or pan, medium heat
1 tablespoon peanut oil

Add plate 1. Fry on each side 2 minutes.
Add cup 1. Simmer 3 minutes one side, 2 minutes other side.

BEAN CURD WITH BLACK BEANS & GARLIC
Tou Fu Dow See Soon Tau

Plate 1
8 oz. canned bean curd cut in 1" cubes. Canned bean curd is firmer than fresh—it can be stir fried in dishes where fresh bean curd would fall apart.

Plate 2
2 scallions cut in 1/4" slices

Cup 1
1 tablespoon stock
1 tablespoon soy sauce
1 teaspoon dry sherry

Wok or pan, medium heat
1-1/2 tablespoons peanut oil
1 teaspoon black beans washed & minced fine
1 clove garlic minced fine

When garlic is golden, add plate 1 and stir for 3-4 minutes until bean curd starts to brown.
Add cup 1 and simmer uncovered 3 minutes.
Add plate 2 and stir about 15 seconds.

BEAN CURD WITH TOMATO & MUSHROOMS

Plate 1
4 oz. mushrooms stems and pieces

Plate 2
8 oz. bean curd (canned) cut in 1" cubes

Plate 3
small tomato 2" diameter, cut in wedges

Cup 1
2 tablespoons stock
1 tablespoon soy sauce
1 teaspoon sugar

Wok or pan, medium heat
1 tablespoon peanut oil
1/2 teaspoon salt

Add plate 1; stir 4 minutes.
Add plate 2 and stir 3 minutes.
Add plate 3 and stir 2 minutes.
Add cup 1 and stir until liquid is reduced by half.
The tomato will add moisture to this dish, but it will not be
enough to worry about.

STIR FRIED LETTUCE WITH GRAVY
Chow Sang Chou Wu

Plate 1
4 oz. canned mushrooms cut in 1/4" slices

Plate 2
1 small lettuce 4" diameter, cut in half, then in 1/4"slices

Cup 1
1/4 cup stock
1 tablespoon corn starch
1 teaspoon soy sauce

Wok or pan, medium heat
1 tablespoon peanut oil
1/2 teaspoon salt

Add plate 1 and stir 5 minutes.
Add plate 2 and stir 2 minutes.
Add cup 1 and stir 2 minutes.

STIR FRIED LETTUCE
Chow Sang Choy

Plate 1
1 head lettuce 5" in diameter, cut in half, then in quarters, then in 1/4" slices to make shreds

Wok or pan, medium heat
1 tablespoon peanut oil
1 clove garlic minced fine
1 slice ginger minced fine

When garlic is golden, add plate 1 and stir 2 minutes.
The lettuce should have a gloss to it and be slightly wilted. If you have never had lettuce this way, you may be hesitant to try it. Please do, and it will become one of your regular recipes. It is quick, cheap, and it has an unusual flavor.

STIR FRIED SPINACH
Chow Bow Choy

Plate 1

4 oz. mushrooms cut in slices 1/8" thick

Plate 2

1 lb. fresh spinach. Wash and remove stalks (save for soup stock). Cut leaves in 1" squares.

Wok or pan, medium heat

1 tablespoon peanut oil

1/2 teaspoon salt

Add plate 1 and stir 3 minutes.
Add plate 2 and stir 2 minutes. The mushrooms may be omitted.

STIR FRIED BEAN SPROUTS
Chow Gna Choy

Plate 1

1 lb. bean sprouts made from mung beans

2 scallions cut in 2" pieces, then in quarters

4 oz. string beans. Remove stems, cut in strips 1/4" wide

Cup 1

1/4 cup stock

1/2 teaspoon sugar

1/2 teaspoon soy sauce

Wok or pan, medium heat

1 tablespoon peanut oil

1/2 teaspoon salt

1 clove garlic minced fine

When garlic is golden, add plate 1 and stir 2 minutes.
Add cup 1. Turn heat to high. Stir 1-2 minutes until most of the liquid is gone.

Vegetables/97

CELLOPHANE NOODLES WITH VEGETABLES
Chow Fun See Choy

Cellophane noodles are known by many names. They are sometimes called bean threads, bean vermicelli, and long rice.

Plate 1
6 black mushrooms about 1-1/2" diameter. Soak in warm water about 30 minutes and cut in strips 1/8" wide.

Plate 2
1/4 cup bamboo shoots cut in strips 2"x1/8"x1/8"
1/4 cup water chestnuts cut in strips same size
1/4 cup green pepper cut in strips same size
1/4 cup onion cut in strips same size

Plate 3
4 oz. package cellophane noodles, soaked in warm water 20 minutes, drained, and cut in 2" pieces
6 pieces baby corn cut in quarters lengthwise

Cup 1
1/2 cup stock

Wok or pan, medium heat
1 tablespoon peanut oil
1/2 teaspoon salt
1 clove garlic minced fine

When garlic is golden, add plate 1 and stir 2 minutes.
Add 1 tablespoon dry sherry and stir 2 minutes.
Add plate 2 and stir 2 minutes.
Add 1 tablespoon soy sauce and cook with cover 2 minutes.
Add plate 3 and stir 1 minute.
Add cup 1 and cover 5 minutes or until most of the gravy is absorbed.

SWEET & SOUR VEGETABLES
Tiem Shuen Choy

Plate 1
1/2 cup carrots cut in 1/4" slices
1/2 cup green peppers cut in 1" squares
1/2 cup bamboo shoots, drained & rinsed in cold water, cut in slices 1/4"x1"x2"

Plate 2
1/2 cup onion in 1/4"slices which are cut in quarters
1/2 cup cabbage cut in 1" squares

Plate 3
1/4 cup cucumber, remove seeds and cut in 1/4" pieces
1/4 cup water chestnuts, cut in 1/4" pieces

Cup 1
1/4 cup wine vinegar
1/2 cup sugar
1/4 cup stock
1 tablespoon corn starch
1 teaspoon soy sauce

Wok or pan, medium heat
1 tablespoon peanut oil
1/2 teaspoon salt
1 clove garlic minced fine

When garlic is golden, add plate 1 and stir 3 minutes.
Add plate 2 and stir 2 minutes.
Add plate 3 and stir 2 minutes.
Add cup 1 and stir until sauce thickens.

SWEET & SOUR CARROTS WITH GREEN PEPPER
Tiem Shuen Hong Low Bok Lot Jiu

Plate 1
1 cup carrots cut in 1/4" slices
1 cup green peppers, cut in 1" squares

Cup 1
2 tablespoons sugar
1 tablespoon wine vinegar
1/2 cup stock

Cup 2
1/2 cup stock
1 tablespoon corn starch

Wok or pan, medium heat
1 tablespoon peanut oil
1/2 teaspoon salt

Stir 15 seconds. Add plate 1 and stir 2 minutes.
Add cup 1, cover for 5 minutes.
Add cup 2 and stir until sauce thickens.

Eggs

Egg dishes are a welcome addition to a Chinese meal. Not only are they colorful, they provide a different texture from meat and poultry dishes. Vegetarians like them and use them frequently.

Don't forget tea eggs which are listed in the Appetizers Chapter.

EGG FOO YOUNG

Place in a mixing bowl:

1/4 cup meat—see below for variations
2 cups bean sprouts, well drained
2 oz. onion, coarsely chopped
2 oz. bok choy or celery shredded 1/8"x2"
1/4 teaspoon salt
dash pepper
2 eggs, stirred but not scrambled

Mix all together. Heat 2" oil in a wok or pan. When bubbles
start to form, use a ladle and pour in one portion of the egg
mixture. When this browns, turn it over and brown the
other side. It should take 3-4 minutes for each side. Repeat
with the balance of the mixture. If you have a large frying
pan or wok,you can do 4 Egg Foo Youngs at one time.
For the gravy, mix the following ingredients in a saucepan:

3/4 cup chicken stock
1 teaspoon soy sauce
1/4 teaspoon salt
1/4 teaspoon sugar
1 tablespoon corn starch

Heat slowly and stir until mixture thickens.
You can use any cooked food in this recipe—vegetable, meat or
seafood. Try 1/2" cubes leftover roast pork, 1/4 cup canned
white mushrooms, or shrimp which have been boiled 3 minutes.

BASIC EGG DISH
Chow Dan

This is similar to Egg Foo Young, but it is stir fried, instead of deep fat fried.

Plate 1
1 piece Lop Chong 3" long, cut in diagonal slices 1/8" thick

Plate 2
1 cup bean sprouts
1 oz. onion, cut in wedge shape
1 oz. mushrooms, canned, in slices 1/8" thick

Cup 1
2 eggs beaten

Wok or pan, medium heat
1 teaspoon oil
1/4 teaspoon salt

Add plate 1 to wok, and stir fry until fat in Lop Chong is transparant, 2-3 minutes.
Add plate 2 and stir fry until onions get soft, 3-4 minutes.
Add cup 1 and let set 1 minute. Then turn over for 1 minute, letting egg set. Stir fry until done, 1-2 minutes.

Substitutions may be made for Lop Chong in plate 1.
Any cooked ingredient may be substituted for the sausage, and all directions remain the same.
Any uncooked ingredient may be substituted, but the cooking time may be longer.

Poultry

If possible, buy whole fresh chickens—they are usually cheaper that way—and cut them up and freeze the pieces in portions that are correct for the recipes. Put aside the giblets, heart, and neck. The combination may be added to the bone pile for soup stock, or you can save the giblets and heart for some of the recipes. Cut the wings off. Then cut off the spurs and tips from the wings and place in bone pile. The pair of wings can be wrapped on one piece of freezer paper. Cut the drum sticks off and wrap. Cut the thighs off and wrap. Bone the breast and wrap in 4 ounce portions. Cut the bones to fit your soup pot. You can make soup immediately and freeze the stock if you wish. Or you can freeze the bones and make soup later on. Use the breast meat for boned chicken recipes and the pieces with bones for unboned chicken recipes.

One 3 lb. chicken will yield 8 oz. wings, 12 oz. drumsticks and thighs, 10 oz. breast meat, and the balance in bones and innards.

It is simplest to package everything in portions that are correct for one recipe, usually 4 oz.

Wings are very popular with Chinese people because of the differences in texture. They can be made into a variety of dishes— they absorb sauces readily. They can also be fried quickly because they are small, 8-10 minutes deep fat fried or 20-30 minutes stir fried.

Long Island Duck or a local product (about 5 lbs.) can be purchased frozen.Defrost the duck in the refrigerator overnight. If not completely defrosted when you are ready to go, drop into cold water and then proceed. Cut off the first joint of the wing, the neck, and if necessary the feet. Use these for soup stock or discard. Continue with the specific duck recipe you are following.

CHICKEN WITH MUSHROOMS
Moo Goo Gai Pan

Plate 1
1 lb. uncooked boned chicken sliced thin, 1/8"

Plate 2
4 oz. canned mushrooms, French or white, sliced 1/8" thick
2 oz. bamboo shoots sliced 1/8" thick
2 oz. water chestnuts sliced 1/8" thick

Cup 1
1/4 cup chicken stock

Cup 2
1/4 cup water
1 tablespoon corn starch

Wok or pan, medium heat
1 tablespoon oil
1/2 teaspoon salt
1 clove garlic minced fine

When garlic turns golden, add plate 1 and stir until chicken turns white.
Add plate 2 and stir 1-2 minutes.
Add cup 1, bring to a boil, then cover 3-4 minutes.
Add cup 2 and stir until mixture thickens slightly. Serve with rice.

This is a good dish for new cooks. It is the easiest to prepare of all the chicken recipes.

PINEAPPLE CHICKEN
Bo Lo Gai

Plate 1
8 oz. uncooked boned chicken sliced thin, 1/8"x1"x2"

Plate 2
4 oz. onion sliced lengthwise
5 water chestnuts sliced 1/8" thick
2 slices canned pineapple cut in eighths

Cup 1
3/4 cup chicken stock
1/2 teaspoon sugar
dash pepper

Cup 2
1 tablespoon pineapple juice
1 tablespoon thick soy sauce
1 tablespoon corn starch
1/4 cup chicken stock

Wok or pan, medium heat
1 tablespoon oil
1/2 teaspoon salt
1 clove garlic minced fine

When garlic starts to turn golden, add plate 1 and stir 3 minutes.
Add 1 tablespoon dry sherry and stir 1 minute.
Add plate 2 and stir 1 minute.
Add cup 1 and bring to a boil. Cover and cook 3-4 minutes.
Uncover and stir in cup 2 until mixture thickens.

CHICKEN WITH LICHEE NUTS
Lichee Gai Kow

Mixing bowl
1/2 cup flour
1 egg
1/4 teaspoon salt
1 tablespoon water
Mix to a smooth paste.

Add 8 oz. raw boned chicken cut in 3/4" to 1" cubes.
Stir until well coated with batter.
Place in heated peanut oil, 375 degrees, for 4-5 minutes, or until golden brown. Drain on a paper towel.

Plate 1
1 cup lichee nuts, canned, without syrup

Cup 1
2 tablespoons water
2 tablespoons corn starch

Wok or pan, medium heat
1/4 teaspoon salt
1 cup sugar
2 tablespoons catsup
4 tablespoons wine vinegar
1 cup water

Stir and bring to a boil. Cook 2 minutes.
Add cup 1 and bring to a boil. Simmer 3 minutes.
Add fried chicken and stir 2 minutes.
Add plate 1 and stir 2 minutes.

LEMON CHICKEN
Ning Mon Gai

Take 1 large chicken breast. Run sharp knife down middle to the bone, but do not cut the bone. Remove skin. Then using thumb nail or back of spoon, force the meat away from the bone.

Make a batter of
1 egg
1/4 cup corn starch
1/2 cup flour
enough water to make a thick batter

Add the chicken meat and stir until meat is well coated. Remove and deep fry at 350 degrees in 2-3 cups peanut oil in a wok. The chicken should be golden colored in 5-6 minutes. Remove and drain on paper towel. Cut in 1" pieces and shape back into original form of breast on a plate lined with lettuce leaves.

In a small saucepan, heat
1/2 cup chicken stock
2 tablespoons lemon juice
1 tablespoon dry sherry
1 tablespoon corn starch
1 tablespoon catsup

When the sauce is hot and begins to thicken, pour over chicken in plate and serve. If you want a very crisp batter, add 1/4 cup water chestnut powder to 1/4 cup of flour to make 1/2 cup, and use this mixture in place of the 1/2 cup flour originally called for in the batter.

STIR FRIED LEMON CHICKEN
Chow Ning Mon Gai

Plate 1
1 lb. uncooked boneless chicken cut in slices 1"x1"
1 tablespoon dry sherry
1 teaspoon soy sauce
2 tablespoons lemon juice
1 tablespoon corn starch
Marinate at least 15 minutes.

Plate 2
4 water chestnuts cut in 1/4" slices
4 lettuce leaves cut in 1/4" strips 2" long
2 oz. bamboo shoots. Drain and slice 1/4" thick, then parboil
for 2-3 minutes

Cup 1
1/4 cup chicken stock
1 tablespoon sugar
1 tablespoon catsup
1 tablespoon lemon juice
1 tablespoon corn starch

Wok or pan, medium heat
1 tablespoon peanut oil
1/4 teaspoon salt
1 clove garlic minced fine

When garlic is golden, add plate 1 and stir 5 minutes until
chicken browns slightly.
Add plate 2 and stir 2 minutes.
Add cup 1 and stir until sauce thickens.

CHICKEN WITH PEANUTS
Gai Far Sung

Plate 1
8 oz. raw boned chicken cut 1/2"x1/2"x1/4"
4 oz. canned mushrooms, stems and pieces
4 oz. bamboo shoots, rinsed and cut 1/2"x1/2"x1/4"
1 green pepper cut 1/2"x1/2"

Plate 2
2 scallions cut in 1/2" pieces
1/2 cup raw peanuts. Pour boiling water over peanuts in bowl,
let stand 5 minutes, drain and add to plate 2.

Cup 1
1/2 cup chicken stock
1 teaspoon soy sauce
1 tablespoon dry sherry
1 teaspoon tabasco or hot pepper sauce

Cup 2
1/4 cup chicken stock
1 tablespoon corn starch

Wok or pan, medium heat
1 tablespoon peanut oil
1 clove garlic minced fine
1 slice ginger root 1/8" thick, minced fine

When garlic is golden, add plate 1 and stir 3-4 minutes until
chicken turns white.
Add plate 2 and stir 1 minute.
Add cup 1 and stir. Cook, covered, for 3 minutes.
Add cup 2 and stir until sauce thickens.

CHICKEN WITH CASHEWS
U Quo Chow Gai Ding

Mixing bowl
8 oz. raw boned chicken cut in 1/2" cubes
1 teaspoon dry sherry
1 teaspoon soy sauce
1 tablespoon corn starch
Marinate at least 15 minutes

Plate 1
4 oz. canned mushrooms stems and pieces
2 oz. water chestnuts cut 1/2" thick
2 oz. bamboo shoots cut in 1/2" cubes, rinsed and
parboiled about 3 minutes
1 oz. snow peas

Plate 2
4 oz. raw cashews. Parboil for 2 minutes or stir fry in 1 tablespoon peanut oil until golden brown.

Cup 1
3/4 cup chicken stock
1 tablespoon corn starch

Wok or pan, medium heat
1 tablespoon peanut oil
1/4 teaspoon salt
1 clove garlic minced fine

When garlic is golden, add mixing bowl and stir until chicken
starts to brown, 3-4 minutes.
Add plate 1 and stir 2 minutes.
Add plate 2 and stir 2 minutes.
Add cup 1 and stir until mixture comes to a boil. Cover 2-3
minutes.
If you prefer a darker gravy, add 1 teaspoon soy sauce to cup 1.

CHICKEN WITH PEPPERS
Chow Gai Lot Jiu

Mixing bowl
8 oz. raw boned chicken cut in 1" cubes
1 tablespoon dry sherry
1 tablespoon soy sauce
1 tablespoon corn starch
Mix well and marinate 15-30 minutes.

Plate 1
1 red sweet pepper
1 green pepper
Both cut in 1" squares

Cup 1
1 tablespoon soy sauce
1 tablespoon dry sherry
1/2 teaspoon sugar
2 tablespoons chicken stock

Cup 2
1/4 cup chicken stock
1 tablespoon corn starch

Wok or pan, medium heat
1 tablespoon peanut oil
1/2 teaspoon salt
1 clove garlic minced fine

When garlic is golden, add mixing bowl and stir until chicken
turns white, about 4 minutes. Return chicken to mixing bowl.
Add 1 tablespoon peanut oil to wok. Add plate 1. Stir 2 minutes.
Add cup 1 and cook with cover for 3 minutes.
Add mixing bowl and cook with cover 2 minutes.
Add cup 2 and stir until sauce thickens.

CHICKEN CHOP SUEY & CHICKEN CHOW MEIN
Gai Chop Suey & Gai Chow Mein

I have been asked to include this recipe by my friends who have been introduced to Chinese food by means of these two dishes. The difference between them is that Chow Mein is served on a layer of fried noodles whereas Chop Suey is served with rice. Some restaurants have a large pot of Chop Suey on the steam table which can be converted to Chow Mein by the substitution of fried noodles. Variations can be made easily by adding other cooked meats or fish to the dish instead of chicken.

Plate 1
8 oz. raw boned chicken sliced 1/4"x1/4"x2"

Plate 2
4 oz. bamboo shoots, rinsed & sliced as above
4 oz. celery, sliced in pieces 2" long then cut in strips 1/4" wide
4 oz. mushrooms stems and pieces

Plate 3
4 oz. bean sprouts
4 oz. onion cut in wedges

Cup 1
3/4 cup chicken stock

Cup 2
1/4 cup chicken stock
1 tablespoon soy sauce
2 tablespoons corn starch

Wok or pan, medium heat
1 tablespoon peanut oil
1 clove garlic minced fine

When garlic is golden, add plate 1 and stir 2 minutes. Add plate 2 and stir 2 minutes. Add cup 1 and cook with cover 10 minutes. Add plate 3 and stir 2-3 minutes. At this point there should be about 1/4 cup stock left. If not, add about 1/4 cup of chicken stock to cup 2. Add cup 2 to the wok. Stir until sauce thickens. Serve with rice for Chop Suey or with noodles for Chow Mein. You can substitute any other raw meat or fish on plate 1.

CHICKEN WITH RICE (DRIED) NOODLES
Chow Gai Sow How Fun

Plate 1

8 oz. raw boned chicken cut in strips 1/4"x1/8"x2"

Plate 2

2 oz. bamboo shoots cut as above
2 oz. cabbage cut as above
2 oz. water chestnuts cut 1/8" thick

Plate 3

6 oz. dried rice noodles, boiled 10 minutes, drained, rinsed with cold water, and drained again.

Cup 1

1/4 cup chicken stock
1 tablespoon soy sauce
1 tablespoon oyster sauce

Wok or pan, medium heat

1 tablespoon peanut oil
1/2 teaspoon salt
1 clove garlic minced fine

When garlic is golden, add plate 1 and stir 3 minutes.
Add plate 2 and stir 2-3 minutes until cabbage starts to wilt.
Add plate 3 and stir 2 minutes.
Add cup 1 and stir. Then cover and cook 2 minutes.
Uncover and stir before serving.

CHICKEN WITH RICE (FRESH) NOODLES
Gai Sow How Fun

Plate 1
8 oz. raw boned chicken sliced 1/8"x1/2"x2"
4 oz. bamboo shoots, rinsed & cut as above

Plate 2
4 oz. water chestnuts cut in 1/8" slices
8 oz. fresh rice noodles cut in strips 1/2"x2"

Cup 1
1 tablespoon dry sherry
1 tablespoon oyster sauce
2 tablespoons chicken stock

Wok or pan, medium heat
1 tablespoon peanut oil
1 clove garlic minced fine

When garlic turns golden, add plate 1 and stir until chicken turns white, 2-3 minutes.
Add plate 2 and stir 3 minutes.
Add cup 1 and cook, covered, 3 minutes. Stir. Raise heat and continue stirring 1 minute.

CHICKEN HEARTS & GIBLETS IN OYSTER SAUCE
Gai Kan Ho Yo

Plate 1
4-6 gizzards. Remove fat and slice 1/4" thick
4-6 hearts. Remove fat and cut in half. Wash in cold water and remove any blood.

Plate 2
2 scallions, white part, in 1" pieces

Cup 1
1-3/4 cup chicken stock
1 tablespoon oyster sauce
1 teaspoon sugar

Wok or pan, medium heat
1 tablespoon peanut oil
1 slice ginger 1/8" thick, minced fine
1 clove garlic, minced fine
1/2 teaspoon salt

When garlic is golden, add plate 1 and stir 3 minutes.
Add 1 tablespoon sherry and stir 1 minute.
Add cup 1 and bring to a boil. Then cover and simmer 20-30 minutes. The sauce should be thick. If it is too thick, add 1 tablespoon water.
Add plate 2. Stir 1 minute.

CHICKEN GIBLETS RED COOKED
Gai Kan See Yeow

Plate 1
4-6 oz. gizzards cleaned and cut in half, then cut half-way through each piece
2-4 black mushrooms, soaked in warm water 30 minutes, cut in strips 1/4" wide

Plate 2
4-6 oz. chicken livers cut in quarters

Plate 3
1 scallion cut in 1/4" pieces

Cup 1
1/4 cup soy sauce
1 teaspoon sugar
1 slice ginger 1/8" minced fine
1/2 cup chicken stock
1 teaspoon dry sherry

Wok or pan, medium heat
1 tablespoon peanut oil
1/2 teaspoon salt
1 clove garlic minced fine

Stir until garlic is golden.
Add plate 1 and stir 5 minutes.
Add cup 1 and simmer 15 minutes covered.
Add plate 2 and simmer 20 minutes covered.
Add plate 3 and stir 1 minute. Serve with rice.

Variation: Instead of stir frying this dish, place cup 1 and plate 1 in a saucepan and simmer, covered, 30 minutes. Add plate 2 and simmer, covered, 10 minutes. Add plate 3, stir on medium heat for 1 minute, and serve.

CHICKEN IN TOMATO SAUCE
Gai Kair Jip

Plate 1
2 lbs. chicken cut in small pieces or
2 lbs. chicken wings or legs separated at the joints

Cup 1
1-1/2 cups chicken stock

Cup 2
1/4 cup stock
1 tablespoon corn starch
1/2 cup catsup

Cup 3
2 scallions cut in 1/4" pieces

Wok or pan, medium heat
2 tablespoons peanut oil
1 teaspoons salt
1 clove garlic minced fine

Heat until garlic is golden. Add plate 1 and stir 1 minute.
Then simmer with cover for 5 minutes.
Add cup 1 and simmer with cover 30 minutes until tender.
Add cup 2 and stir. If there is too much liquid in wok, increase
the heat and cook until mixture begins to thicken.
Add cup 3. Stir and serve.

GOLDEN CHICKEN
Gom Gai

1 cup chicken stock
1 chicken (2-3 lbs.) cut in 8 pieces or
6 chicken wings and 6 drumsticks

Place in a wok or soup pot. Add

1/8 cup soy sauce
1 teaspoon sugar
dash of dry ginger or 1 slice fresh ginger 1/8" thick minced fine
1 teaspoon dry sherry

Bring to a boil. Then simmer, covered, 20-30 minutes.
Turn chicken several times so that it cooks evenly.

CHINESE FRIED CHICKEN
Jar Doo Guy

After you have made chicken stock (see the Soup Chapter), take the cooked chicken, cut it apart at the joints and deep fry it at 375 degrees until the outside is crisp, about 6-8 minutes.

Or you can remove the bones from the cooked chicken and dip the meat into the following batter
1 egg
1/2 cup flour
1 tablespoon cold water
1/2 teaspoon salt

Deep fry the batter-dipped pieces at 375 degrees until golden.

BARBEQUED CHICKEN
Shu Gai

Clean a 3 lb. fryer and split in halves or quarters. Place in an ovenproof dish with sides at least 2" high. Pour the following marinade, which has been put through the blender for 3 minutes at high speed, over the chicken.

3/4 cup soy sauce
2 cloves garlic
1/4 cup sugar
1 oz. onion
2 tablespoons catsup (Del Monte with pineapple vinegar)
1 slice lemon
1 slice fresh ginger or 1/8 teaspoon dry ginger
3 tablespoons dry sherry

Cover the dish with plastic to prevent evaporation. Let stand at least 2 hours or all day if possible. Turn and baste 2-3 times. Preheat the oven to 350 degrees. Bake chicken 45 minutes at this temperature, basting twice. Raise the temperature to 450 degrees until done, about 15-20 minutes. The combination of time and temperature works well.

You can grill the chicken in a preheated covered grill for 60-90 minutes. Baste twice.

Or you can grill the chicken 5" above the hot coals and grill on each side until chicken is done, about 40 minutes in all. Baste every 15 minutes or so.

If you want a very crisp skin, mix 1 tablespoon marinade with 1 tablespoon honey and use the mixture on the last basting for any of the above methods.

CHICKEN WINGS WITH OYSTER SAUCE
Ho Yo Gai Yick

Plate 1
1 lb. chicken wings (5-6 wings) cleaned, with tips cut off

Cup 1
1 cup chicken stock
2 tablespoons oyster sauce
1 teaspoon sugar
1 teaspoon sherry

Wok or pan, medium heat
2 tablespoons oil
1/2 teaspoon salt
1/4" slice ginger root minced fine or 1/4 teaspoon dry ginger

Add plate 1 and fry the wings until brown.
Add cup 1 and simmer, covered, 15-20 minutes.
Uncover and cook 5 minutes to reduce amount of sauce.
When the sauce thickens and sticks to the wings, serve.

CHICKEN WINGS, RED COOKED
See Yeow Gai Yick

Place about 2 lbs of chicken wings (8-12 wings) in a wok.
Add

1/2 cup soy sauce
1 teaspoon sugar
1 slice ginger 1/8" thick minced fine
1/4 cup chicken stock
1 teaspoon dry sherry

Bring to a boil. Simmer with cover 20-30 minutes until sauce is thickened. Add 1 scallion cut in 1/4" pieces and serve.

CHICKEN WINGS IN 5 SPICE
Ng Heung Fun Gai Yick

Plate 1
2 lbs. chicken wings

Cup 1
1-1/2 cup water
2 tablespoons soy sauce
1 tablespoon dry sherry
1 teaspoon sugar
1/8 to 1/2 teaspoon of 5 spice

Wok or pan, medium heat
1 tablespoon oil
1/2 teaspoon salt
1 clove garlic minced fine

When garlic turns golden, add plate 1 and stir 5 minutes until chicken wings are brown.
Add cup 1, bring to a boil; cover and simmer 30 minutes.
The liquid should be almost all gone and a thin coating should remain on the wings. This is a finger dish. It can be served cold or warm.

CHICKEN WINGS IN BLACK BEAN SAUCE
Dow See Gai Yick

Plate 1
2 lbs. chicken wings, cut at joints in 3 sections

Plate 2
1 scallion cut in 1" pieces

Cup 1
3/4 cup chicken stock
1 teaspoon sugar

Cup 2
1/4 cup water
1 teaspoon thick soy sauce

1 tablespoon corn starch

Wok or pan, medium heat
2 tablespoons peanut oil
1 teaspoon salt
2 cloves garlic minced
1 tablespoon black beans minced

Heat until garlic turns golden. Add plate 1 and brown wings.
Add cup 1. Bring to a boil. Simmer with cover 20 minutes.
Add cup 2 until thickened slightly. Add plate 2 and serve.

CURRIED CHICKEN
Gar Lee Chow Gai

Plate 1
2-3 lb. chicken cut in 1-1/2" pieces. It is easiest to have a butcher
do this with a band saw. Wash the chicken before using to
remove any possible bone splinters from the band saw.

Plate 2
8 oz. potato cut in 1" cubes

Plate 3
4 oz. onion, wedge cut
8 oz. canned mushrooms or black mushrooms, soaked & cut

Cup 1
3 teaspoons curry powder
2 cups stock

Wok or pan, medium heat
3 tablespoons peanut oil
1/4 teaspoon salt
1 clove garlic minced fine

When garlic is golden, add plate 1 and stir 10 minutes until
chicken is lightly browned.
Add cup 1 and simmer with cover 30 minutes.
Add plate 2 and simmer with cover 20 minutes.
Add plate 3 and simmer with cover 10 minutes. There should be
about 1/4 cup liquid left. If there is much more liquid, increase
heat for a few minutes with cover off. Serve with rice.

SMOKED CHICKEN
Hsun Gai

Mention this dish to Chinese gourmets and very few will know what you are talking about. It is rarely served in restaurants though some will special order it for you. It is far more likely to be served at private parties or in Chinese social clubs. The best place to find smoked chicken so that you can sample it is at a Chinese delicatessen or grocery store. In China Town there are such stores with trays of unusual foods in the window—chicken feet, duck feet, pigs' stomach, and so on. Some stores will sell you food to take out whereas others have tables where you can eat the food right on the spot.

Wherever you find smoked chicken, you will like it. The flavor is extraordinary. It is not difficult to make, just troublesome because of the smoke which permeates everything in the house and lingers for weeks thereafter. It is easier to cook out of doors and I suggest doing just that in the summertime. In the winter, the only recourse is to shut off the kitchen from the rest of the house and to open all the kitchen windows until you are through smoking.

I give two methods of cooking and two methods of smoking. Use any combination of the two methods until you find one that suits you best.

Cooking method 1
Take a 2-3 lb. fryer, clean it, remove giblets and all visible fat. Pat the chicken dry (it should be a whole bird), then brush with soy sauce, and let dry in the air. Place the bird in a large glass ovenproof dish, which you can then place in a steamer (top section) and steam for 45 minutes. Place the chicken in a colander and drain the soup off. It can be used for stock.

Cooking method 2
Take a 2-3 lb. fryer, clean it, remove giblets and all visible fat. Place the whole bird into a soup pot. Add the giblets and cover the bird with water. Bring to a boil and then simmer, with a cover, for 45 minutes. Remove chicken and drain off soup stock.

Smoking method 1
Use a large cast iron pot with a tight fitting lid. Place a wire trivet at the bottom of this pot. Take an old ceramic or ovenproof glass plate and put it on the trivet; the smoking process will discolor the plate, so choose a plate that doesn't matter to you. Put the chicken which has been boiled or steamed on this plate.

Sprinkle 2 tablespoons of brown sugar and 2 tablespoons black tea (Oolong works fine) on the bottom of the pot. Turn the heat to medium. As soon as smoke begins to seep out of the pot, turn the heat down to low for 15-20 minutes. Use a kitchen fan if you have one, and make sure the room is adequately ventilated.

Smoking method 2
Line the bottom of a wok or pan with a few layers of heavy aluminum foil. Let the foil hang over both sides so that you will have enough to go over the chicken.

Sprinkle 2 tablespoons each brown sugar and black tea leaves on the bottom of the foil. Place the trivet on top of the sugar and tea, an old plate on the trivet, and the boiled or steamed chicken on the plate. Wrap the whole thing securely in foil. Set heat at low and cook for 10 minutes. Lower heat still more and cook 10 minutes.Serve hot or cold.

The wok does the job faster than the cast iron pot, but the cast iron pot gets better results. This is my opinion. Try both methods and make up your own mind.

PEKING DUCK
Peking Op

This is a famous Mandarin dish. Chinese chefs tell me that in Peking where the dish originates the ducks are particularly fine. The climate in Peking is also favorable. Since it is cool there much of the time, cooks can hang the ducks up to dry outside.

Here the chefs have to make do with local ducks or Long Island ducks, and they are forced to hang the birds up to dry in a walk in cooler or a second refrigerator.

To duplicate the dish at home, you need an outside porch when the weather is cool or a second refrigerator. You will also need some patience. The dish takes a long time but is well worth it.

Defrost the duck (about 5 lbs.) according to directions given at the beginning of this chapter. Cut off the neck, feet, and first joint of the wings and use these for soup stock. Tie a double thickness of white cord around the neck of the duck, or run a double thickness of white cord through the body cavity. Lower the duck by means of the cord into a pot of boiling water. Let the duck remain submerged in the boiling water for 5 minutes. If your pot is too small, let the bird cook on one side for 5 minutes, and then turn it over to cook on the other side for 5 minutes.

Remove the duck and let it hang and drain a few minutes over the sink. When it is cool enough to handle, work the skin between the fingers with a pinching motion going over the duck completely. This makes the skin looser and allows the fat to drain better so that you end up with a crisp textured skin.

Hang the duck up by the cord in a refrigerator or a screened porch or in front of a fan. After 4 hours, coat the duck with a pastry brush dipped into the following mixture:

1 cup warm water
2 tablespoons honey
1 tablespoon dry sherry
1 teaspoon soy sauce

Hang the duck up to dry once more. When the skin is dry, warm the above mixture up a bit, and give the duck a second coating.

128/Poultry

Place a bowl under the duck to catch all the drippings. When the duck is cool, brush with soy sauce.

When the duck has hung a total of 8 hours, place it on a rack in a shallow roasting pan for 1-1/2 hours at 300 degrees, turning every 30 minutes. Use tongs to turn the duck so that you do not break the skin. Or take a bit of clean wire and tie it around the neck with a ring at the end so that you can lift the duck off the rack to turn it.

While the duck is roasting in the oven, you can make pancakes if you like. See the Index for page number. Make a double batch, since it is better to have left over pancakes than left over duck.

When the duck is ready, place it on a carving board and remove all the skin. Cut the skin in strips about 1"x2" and stack it on one plate. Cut the rest of the duck off the bone in pieces the same size, 1/8" thick. Stack on another plate.

Take scallions, cut off the roots, and cut the pieces of stalk into 3" lengths. Cut through these 3" lengths 1" lengthwise, and crisp in ice water so that they form paint brushes. Place one of these paint brushes in an individual serving bowl beside a few tablespoons of hoisin sauce.

Each person takes a pancake and then uses a scallion brush to coat the pancake with hoisin sauce. A piece of duck skin or meat is placed on the pancake and the whole thing is rolled up.

If your friends like scallions, they will surely include their paint brushes in their pancakes. Make plenty of scallions.

The duck bones can be used for soup stock.

PRESSED BONELESS DUCK
Wor Shu Op

This is my favorite dish along with Lobster Cantonese. When I am trying out a new restaurant, I order boneless duck because there are no variations of ingredients or method possible—it is a real test of a chef's skill. They key ingredient is water chestnut powder which keeps the crust of the duck crisp.

Defrost a 4-5 lb. Long Island duck or equivalent and remove giblets. Place duck in large pot and cover with water. Add

1 teaspoon salt
1 tablespoon soy sauce
1 star anise (or 8 points if broken)
1 slice ginger root 1/8" thick, minced

Bring to a boil. Then reduce heat to medium. Cover and simmer for 2 hours. Remove duck and let cool. Remove skin by cutting down backbone. Keep skin in as large pieces as possible. Then remove meat and place in a 3/4" layer on a Pyrex plate. Spread a layer of water chestnut powder over the duck meat about 1/8" thick. Lay the skin over the water chestnut powder. Put another layer of water chestnut powder over the skin. Take another Pyrex plate (the same size) and put it on top of the first dish. Press down. If necessary, place a weight on top of the second plate—a 5 lb. bag of sugar will work fine. After 20-30 minutes, place in a steamer for 30 minutes. Let cool. Cut in strips 2" wide. Deep fry these strips until the crust is brown, 350 degrees for 10 minutes.

Cut these strips into pieces 1" wide and place on a serving tray which has been lined with lettuce leaves.

Combine the following ingredients in a small sauce pan:
1 tablespoon corn starch
1 cup chicken or duck stock
3 tablespoons oyster sauce
and cook, stirring, until thick. Pour over the duck on the platter, and top with almonds which have been chopped in 1/8" pieces.

Some restaurants use a sweet and sour sauce which is also good.
1/4 cup wine vinegar
1 teaspoon soy sauce
1/4 cup catsup
1/2 cup chicken or duck stock
1/2 cup sugar
1 tablespoon corn starch
Combine in a small saucepan and cook, stirring, until thick.
Pour over duck and top with chopped almonds or cashews.

Some ducks will make 2 serving plates 8"x8". Anything that cannot be eaten should be frozen after steaming or after frying for 2-3 minutes and used later.

After meat is removed from the duck, the bones can be used for duck soup or stock with the wing tips, neck and giblets. The water that was used to cook the duck initially is too strong for soup stock for most people, but it can be used for gravy. Strain it through cheesecloth and refrigerate or freeze.

PINEAPPLE DUCK
Bo Lo Op

Since there are usually a few portions left over from the preceding recipe, this companion recipe is very useful. It is sufficiently different that both dishes can be served the same day without boredom.

Use leftover portions of Wor Shu Op, or prepare the duck as for Wor Shu Op. Deep fry the pieces at 350 degrees for 10 minutes until crust is golden. Place on bed of shredded lettuce.
For a sauce, use the following mixture which has been heated until thick:
1/4 cup wine vinegar
1/2 cup sugar
1/2 cup chicken or duck stock
1 tablespoon catsup
2 tablespoons pineapple syrup
1 tablespoon corn starch

After the sauce is cooked, add
2 slices pineapple
6 lichee nuts, canned
6 maraschino cherries

Cook 2 minutes more and pour over duck on lettuce shreds. This dish is specially colorful due to the red, white, and yellow fruits against the golden color of the duck. It is another dish to serve on a special occasion.

Beef

Flank steak is the most economical cut of beef available for Chinese cooking—it has no bones and a minimum of fat. The cut runs between 3/4" to 1-1/2" thick and, when cut in strips lengthwise, then crosswise into narrows slices, the grain is exposed so that the meat absorbs any marinade readily. It also is a very tender cut of meat. It may cost a trifle more, but it is easy to handle and it has no waste.

I usually take a whole flank, and cut it into strips lengthwise, 1-1/2" to 2" wide. Then I cut these strips into 4 oz. lengths. so that each length constitutes a portion or a single recipe. I wrap each 4 oz. piece individually in plastic freezer wrap and freeze it, making sure it lies flat during the freezing process so that when it is taken out of the freezer it is an oblong piece, not a freely shaped form. When the beef is needed, I take the piece out of the freezer and let it stand at room temperature for 15 minutes. Then I slice it thinly while it is still slightly frozen. When the beef is firm this way, the slicing is simple.

For ground beef, I buy chuck steak and grind it myself in a meat grinder with a coarse blade and 1/4" holes. Then I form the beef into 4 oz. patties (in a hamburger press). Then I lay the patties on a baking sheet or tray covered with plastic film and freeze them until firm. They lie flat this way. After they are frozen, I wrap them individually with plastic wrap.

Shin beef is used by American cooks primarily for soups and stews. The Chinese use it in a stew with all its bone and marrow to create a wonderfully flavored stock. Chicken stock or chicken bones is added to soften the strong beef flavor for some recipes.

PEPPER STEAK
Lot Jiu Ngow Yoke

Plate 1
1 lb. beef—flank, chuck, or sirloin—sliced thin, 1/8"x1-1/2"

Plate 2
1 large green pepper cut in 1" pieces
1 onion, about 2 oz., cut in 8ths.

Cup 1
1 teaspoon sugar
1 teaspoon sherry
1/2 cup chicken stock
dash pepper

Cup 2
2 tablespoons corn starch
1 tablespoon thick soy sauce
1/2 cup water

Wok or pan, medium heat
2 tablespoons oil
1 teaspoon salt
1 large clove garlic, minced fine

When garlic turns golden, add plate 1. Stir and cook 2-3 minutes until beef begins to brown.
Add cup 1 and cook 2 minutes.
Add plate 2. Stir and then simmer, covered, 3 minutes.
Stir cup 2 until mixture is smooth. Then add to wok. Cook until mixture thickens, about 2 minutes.

If you prefer the green pepper softer to the bite, drop the pieces into boiling water 2-3 minutes, drain, and then proceed with directions.

BEEF WITH ASPARAGUS
Gna Shun Ngow Yoke

Mixing bowl
1 tablespoon corn starch
1 tablespoon dry sherry
1 tablespoon soy sauce
8 oz. flank steak sliced 1/8"x1/2"x2"
Marinate 15 minutes.

Plate 1
1 lb. asparagus. Discard inedible bottoms. Cut off tips and reserve for plate 2. The remaining stalks should be cut in 1/8"x1" pieces, and parboiled 2-3 minutes.

Plate 2
Asparagus tips
4 scallions cut in 1"pieces

Cup 1
1/2 cup chicken stock

Cup 2
1/4 cup chicken stock
1 tablespoon corn starch
1 teaspoon soy sauce

Wok or pan, high heat
1 tablespoon peanut oil
1/2 teaspoon salt
1 clove garlic minced fine

When garlic is golden, add mixing bowl and stir until meat starts to brown, 3-4 minutes.
Add plate 1 and stir 2 minutes.
Add cup 1 and cook with cover 2 minutes.
Add plate 2 and cook, stirring, 1 minute.
Add cup 2 and stir until sauce thickens.

BEEF WITH BROCCOLI
Ngow Yoke Gai Lon Choy

Mixing bowl
1 tablespoon corn starch
1 tablespoon dry sherry
1 tablespoon soy sauce
8 oz. flank steak sliced 1/8"x1/2"x2"
Marinate at least 15 minutes.

Plate 1
Cut off flowers at top of broccoli and reserve for plate2.
Cut remainder in pieces 1/2" long across stalk. Parboil 1 minute.

Plate 2
Flower tops of broccoli cut in 1/2" pieces

Cup 1
1/2 cup chicken stock

Cup 2
1/4 cup water
1 tablespoon corn starch

Wok or pan, high heat
1 tablespoon peanut oil
1/2 teaspoon salt
1 clove garlic minced fine

When garlic is golden, add mixing bowl and stir until meat
browns, 3-4 minutes.
Add plate 1 and stir 2 minutes.
Add plate 2 and stir 1 minute.
Add cup 1 and cook with cover 2 minutes.
Add cup 2 and stir until sauce thickens.

BEEF WITH STRING BEANS
Ngow Yoke Chow Dow Jay

Mixing bowl
1 tablespoon corn starch
1 tablespoon dry sherry
1 tablespoon soy sauce
8 oz. flank steak, sliced 1/8"x1/2"x2"
Marinate at least 15 minutes.

Plate 1
8 oz. string beans. Remove string and cut or break in pieces about 2" long
2 oz. canned mushrooms, stems and pieces
8 oz. bamboo shoots. Drain and rinse. Then cut in pieces 1/8"x 1/2"x2".
2 oz. water chestnuts cut 1/8" thick

Cup 1
1/2 cup chicken stock

Cup 2
1/4 cup stock
1 tablespoon corn starch

Wok or pan, medium heat
1 tablespoon peanut oil
1/2 teaspoon salt
1 clove garlic minced fine

When garlic is golden, add mixing bowl and stir 2-3 minutes until meat is browned lightly.
Add plate 1 and stir 2 minutes.
Add cup 1 and cook with cover 2 minutes.
Add cup 2 and stir until sauce thickens.

BEEF WITH CUCUMBER
Wong Gar Ngow Yoke

Mixing bowl
1 lb. flank steak sliced 1/8" thick
2 tablespoons soy sauce
2 tablespoons corn starch
Let marinate 15 minutes after mixing.

Plate 1
2 medium cucumbers. Wash and peel lengthwise with a potato
peeler so that there are white and green strips running vertically.
Cut in half lengthwise and use a teaspoon to remove seeds.
Cut slices 1/8".

Cup 1
1/4 cup chicken stock
1 teaspoon sherry

Put 2 tablespoons oil in wok. Add plate 1, stir 3 minutes until
cucumber is opaque. Place cucumbers back on plate 1.
Add 2 tablespoons oil to wok. Add mixing bowl and stir 3-5
minutes until meat browns. Add plate 1 and stir fry 1-2 minutes.
Add cup 1 and cook, covered, 2 minutes.

BEEF WITH PEAS
Chang Dow Ngow

Plate 1
1 lb. beef, raw, in 1" cubes
4 oz. onion chopped coarsely

Plate 2
4 oz. onion cut lengthwise
4 oz. frozen or fresh peas
2 stalks celery cut in 1" pieces

Cup 1
3/4 cup chicken stock
1 tablespoon soy sauce

Cup 2
1/4 cup cold water
1 tablespoon corn starch

Wok or pan, medium heat
2 tablespoons oil

Add plate 1 and brown meat.
Add cup 1. Cover and cook 10 minutes.
Add plate 2 and stir for 2 minutes.
Add cup 2. Stir until mixture thickens. Serve with rice.

SHREDDED BEEF WITH CHILI PEPPERS

Plate 1
1 stalk celery, about 2 oz., cut in matchsticks
2 oz. carrots cut in matchsticks
2 oz. bamboo shoots cut in matchsticks
2 oz. onion cut in thin slices crossways, then in half so that
pieces are thin like matches but curved
2 hot peppers. Remove seeds and cut in thin strips.

Mixing bowl
1 lb. lean meat (I prefer flank steak) cut in 1/8"x2" strips, then
cut again in strips 1/8" wide.
3 tablespoons soy sauce
1 tablespoon dry sherry
1 teaspoon sugar
1 slice ginger 1/8" thick, minced fine
Mix and let marinate a minimum of 1/2 hour.

Cup 1, optional if you want a gravy
1/2 cup chicken stock
1 tablespoon corn starch

Wok or pan, medium heat
1 tablespoon peanut oil

Add plate 1. Stir 3 minutes. Return to plate 1.
Add 1 tablespoon oil to wok. Add meat only from mixing
bowl. Stir 5 minutes.
Add liquid from mixing bowl.
Add plate 1. Stir until most of liquid is absorbed, 2 minutes.
If you want a gravy, add cup 1 now and stir until gravy is
translucent.

BEEF WITH OYSTER SAUCE
Ho Yo Ngow

Plate 1
3/4 lb. flank steak sliced 1/8"x2"
4 oz. canned mushrooms drained

Plate 2
1 scallion cut in 1/4" pieces

Cup 1
2 tablespoons oyster sauce
1/4 teaspoon salt
1/2 teaspoon sugar
1/2 cup chicken stock

Cup 2
1 tablespoon corn starch
3 tablespoons water or chicken stock

Wok or pan, medium heat
1 tablespoon peanut oil
1 clove garlic minced fine

Add plate 1 and stir fry 3-5 minutes until meat browns lightly.
Add 1 tablespoon dry sherry and stir 1 minute.
Add cup 1 and stir 3 minutes.
Add cup 2 until sauce thickens slightly.
Add plate 2 and stir 1 minute. Serve with rice.

BEEF SHIN OR BEEF SHANK
Ngow Gin

This cut is usually used for soup. This recipe, however, uses it for a hearty yet light stew. The preparation is minimal.

Plate 1
1-2 lb. shank meat cut in 1" cubes. Include the bones—they will flavor the stock and the marrow is good to eat.

Plate 2
4 oz. onion, tangerine cut
4 oz. carrot in slices 1/4" thick
4 oz. cabbage in 1" squares

Cup 1
2 tablespoons soy sauce
2 tablespoons dry sherry
1 tablespoon brown sugar
2 black mushrooms. Break in quarters and remove stem. Rinse in cold water.

Cup 2
1 cup chicken stock

Wok or pan, medium heat
1 tablespoon peanut oil
1 clove garlic minced fine
1 slice ginger 1/8" thick, minced fine

When garlic is golden, add plate 1 and stir 5 minutes.
Add cup 1 and cook with cover 10 minutes.
Add cup 2 and cook with cover 45 minutes.
Check occasionally to make sure liquid has not evaporated.
Add plate 2 and cook with cover 10 minutes.

Other vegetables can be added if desired—bamboo shoots and water chestnuts are good choices.

STEAMED GROUND BEEF
Jing Ngow Yoke

Mixing bowl
8 oz. ground beef (lean)
2 oz. onion minced fine
2 oz. water chestnuts minced fine
2 tablespoons soy sauce
2 tablespoons dry sherry
1/8 teaspoon pepper

Mix well and place in 8-10" ovenproof bowl. Place in steamer for 20 minutes. This dish will pick up moisture from the steam which will produce a light colored sauce with wonderful flavor. The meat has a nice texture and the water chestnuts give it a good crunch.

STIR FRIED GROUND BEEF

Plate 1
8 oz. lean ground beef

Plate 2
2 oz. onion in pea size pieces
2 oz. water chestnuts cut in pea size pieces
2 oz. bamboo shoots in pea size pieces
2 oz. cabbage cut in 1/4"x2" strips

Cup 1
1 tablespoon soy sauce
2 tablespoons dry sherry

Cup 2
1/2 tablespoon oyster sauce

Wok or pan, medium heat
1 tablespoon peanut oil
1 clove garlic minced fine

When garlic is golden, add plate 1 and stir to break up meat. Meat should brown 3-4 minutes. Add plate 2 and stir 2 minutes. Add cup 1 and stir. Cook with cover 3 minutes. Uncover and add cup 2.

SWEET & SOUR MEATBALLS
Tiem Shuen Ngow Yoke Kow

Mix together
1 lb. lean ground beef
1 oz. minced onion
1 oz. water chestnuts minced fine
1 tablespoon soy sauce
1 teaspoon dry sherry

Form into small balls, the size of a walnut, about 18 to the lb. Beat 1 egg with a chopstick. Drop meatballs into the egg mixture and then roll in 3/4 cup corn starch until coated Deep fry the meatballs in peanut oil at 350 degrees until brown. Keep warm.

Plate 1
1 small green pepper cut in 1" squares

Plate 2
1/4 cup pineapple tidbits
1/4 cup mixed sweet pickles

Cup 1
1/4 cup wine vinegar
1/2 cup sugar
1/4 cup chicken stock
1 tablespoon catsup
1/2 teaspoon salt
2 tablespoons syrup from pineapple
1 teaspoon juice from pickles
1-1/2 tablespoons corn starch
1 tablespoon soy sauce

Wok or pan, medium heat
1 tablespoon peanut oil

Add plate 1 and stir fry 2 minutes.
Add cup 1 and simmer until mixture thickens.
Add plate 2 and stir 1 minute. Pour over meatballs on serving plate. Top with 2 tablespoons of shredded cocoanut.

BEEF WITH CELLOPHANE NOODLES
Ngow Yoke Chow Fun See

Mixing bowl

8 oz. flank steak, sliced 1/8" thick, then in shreds 1/8" wide by 2"
1 tablespoon dry sherry
1/2 teaspoon sugar
1 tablespoon soy sauce
Mix together and let stand at least 5 minutes.

Plate 2
4 oz. (1 package) cellophane noodles

Plate 3
4 oz. bamboo shoots 1/8"x1/8"x2"
4 oz. celery cut 1/8"x1/8"x2"

Cup 1
1 cup chicken stock

Cup 2
1/2 cup chicken stock
1 tablespoon soy sauce
1 scallion cut in shreds 2" long

Wok or pan, medium heat
1 tablespoon peanut oil

Add plate 1 and stir fry 5 minutes. Return beef to plate 1.
Place plate 2 and cup 1 in wok. Simmer with cover 10 minutes.
Check liquid to make sure mixture does not burn.
Add plate 3 and cook with cover 3 minutes. If there is not enough
liquid in wok, add 1/4 cup more.
Add cup 2 and stir 2 minutes.
Add plate 1. Liquid should be almost all absorbed.

If you have trouble when you first try this dish, you can simmer
the cellophane noodles in 4 cups of water 10 minutes before adding them to the wok. Cup 1 will not be needed.

Pork

For most of these pork dishes, you can use fresh bork butt or pork loin. Cut the meat off the bone, save the bones for soup stock (especially good when cooked along with chicken bones), and slice the meat in pieces 4"x2"x2". This is the ideal size for making roast pork, or other dishes. Freeze flat on a tray and then package the pieces individually in freezer wrap. When you need a portion, remove from the freezer and let it thaw 20 minutes— it will be just firm enough to slice easily.

On sparerib dishes, buy the cut from the tip end of the rib, back to the backbone, but not including the backbone If you wish to freeze spareribs, do it after roasting, not before. Raw spareribs dry out too much in the freezer.

On pigs' feet, watch out for sales and stock up. Have your butcher split these down the middle between the hooves. It will make the handling easier. Be sure to wash the meat to remove bone fragments.

Have your butcher slice smoked pork or ham into 1/4" or 1/2" slices. You can cut these into 4 oz. portions. Lay them flat on a tray. Freeze flat and then wrap individually for future use.

ROAST PORK
Char Shu

Take a 2-3 lb. pork butt or loin. Trim off fat and cut in strips 1" thick, 3" wide, and about 6-7" long. Place in bottom of a glass dish.

Mix the following ingredients together for a marinade, or put through blender.

1 teaspoon sugar
1 teaspoon honey
3 tablespoons soy sauce
1 clove garlic, minced fine
1 tablespoon dry sherry
1/4 teaspoon 5-spice, optional

Pour the marinade over the pork and cover the dish with plastic wrap to keep the meat from drying out. Place in refrigerator. Turn the meat over in 2 hours and cover the dish once more. Leave the meat in the marinade in the refrigerator a minimum of 3 hours—the dish will taste much better if you leave it in the marinade all day or all night.

Place the pork on a rack in a baking pan with 1 cup of water in it (to keep meat from drying out in the oven).
Bake in preheated 350 degree oven for 30 minutes.
Remove the pork strips from rack with metal tongs and dip in marinade once more. Return to rack in oven and bake for 30 minutes more.

When pork is done, cut on an angle across grain 1/4" thick and serve with hot mustard sauce or duck sauce.

If any is left over, it can be stored in the refrigerator about 1 week. Or it can be frozen for future use. To reheat roast pork, place it under the broiler for 4 minutes with a basting of drippings or soup stock.

TWICE COOKED PORK, MANDARIN STYLE

Take 1 lb. of pork, cut from loin or shoulder. Trim fat off. Add 6 dried black mushrooms. Cover with water and simmer, with cover, for 30 minutes. Remove pork, let cool, and cut in 1"x2" pieces. Remove mushrooms and cut in strips. Save the broth for soup or stock.

Plate 1
Pork from above
Mushrooms from above
1 green pepper in 1"x2" pieces
4 oz. bamboo shoots sliced 1/8"x1"x2"
1 cup cabbage in 1"x2" pieces
4 oz. onion cut in wedges

Cup 1
1/4 cup stock
1 tablespoon soy sauce
1 tablespoon dry sherry
1 tablespoon hoisin sauce, optional but worth having
1 teaspoon sugar

Wok or pan, medium heat
2 tablespoons peanut oil
1 clove garlic minced fine
1 slice ginger minced fine

Heat until garlic is golden. Add plate 1 and stir 2 minutes. Cook with cover 2 minutes.
Add cup 1 and stir 2 minutes. Cook with cover 3 minutes.
If you wish a thicker sauce, you can add 1 tablespoon corn starch to the soy sauce and sherry mixture.

HOT SLICED PORK

This dish, at first, looks like Twice Cooked Pork. But it has some subtle differences which make the completed dish entirely different.

Take 1 lb. of pork cut from loin or shoulder. Trim off fat. Cover with water. Bring to a boil and then simmer, with cover, for 30 minutes. Remove pork and let cool. Slice in 1/8"x1"x2" pieces. Some of the stock may be used in this recipe. The remainder can be saved for future use.

Plate 1
Strips of pork cut as above
1 green pepper in 1"x2" pieces
1/4 cup bamboo shoots rinsed and cut 1/8" strips
1 cup cabbage in 1"x2" pieces

Plate 2
1/4 cup water chestnuts
1 piece bean curd 3"x3". Gently fry bean curd on both sides in a tablespoon of oil. Add 1 teaspoon soy sauce and fry on both sides once more. Remove from pan and cut in 1/8" slices, then in half, so that the pieces are 1/8"x1"x1-1/2".

Cup 1
1/4 cup chicken stock or pork stock or mixture of the two
1 tablespoon soy sauce
1 teaspoon sugar
1/2 teaspoon tabasco sauce or hot pepper sauce. Increase this amount if you wish.

Wok or pan, medium heat
2 tablespoons peanut oil
1/2 teaspoon salt
1 clove garlic minced fine

When garlic is golden, add plate 1 and stir 2 minutes. Then simmer with cover for 2 minutes.
Add cup 1 and stir fry 2 minutes.
Add plate 2 and cover 3 minutes to steam
If you want a thicker gravy, add 1/4 cup stock mixed with 1/2 tablespoon corn starch and stir until gravy thickens.

BARBEQUED SPARERIBS
Shew Pai Gut

Take one rack of ribs, 2-3 lbs., and trim most of fat off.
Mix together the following marinade in a blender:

6 tablespoons soy sauce
4 tablespoons hoisin sauce, optional
4 tablespoons sherry
2 tablespoons brown sugar
3 cloves garlic
2 tablespoons catsup

Pour marinade over the ribs and let stand no less than 30 minutes,
overnight preferably.

Place the ribs on a rack in a shallow roasting pan with 1 cup of
water at the bottom--it will prevent the ribs from drying out.
Bake the ribs in a preheated 350 degree oven for 1 hour. Baste
every 15 minutes.

Mix 2 tablespoons of leftover marinade with 1 tablespoon
honey and baste the ribs. Bake at 450 degrees 10-15 minutes
longer.

Serve with hot mustard sauce or duck sauce. This is a finger
dish.

SPARERIBS WITH PINEAPPLE
Bo Lo Pai Gut

Have your butcher cut 1 lb. of spareribs in 1-1/2" pieces with a bandsaw. Then you can separate them with a knife. Add water to cover, then bring to a boil, and simmer with cover for 20 minutes. Drain and place on a plate.

Cup 1
1/2 cup pineapple juice. Use juice from can containing pineapple.
1/2 cup chicken stock
1/4 cup wine vinegar
1/4 cup sugar
1 tablespoon soy sauce

Cup 2
1 cup pineapple chunks
2-3 cherries, maraschino, cut in half. Optional.

Cup 3
1/4 cup stock
1 tablespoon corn starch

Wok or pan, medium heat
1 tablespoon peanut oil
1 clove garlic minced fine

When garlic is golden, add spareribs and stir fry 2 minutes. Add cup 1 and turn heat to low so that mixture simmers gently for 10 minutes. Add more stock if needed.

Add cup 2 and cook with cover 2 minutes.
Add cup 3 and stir until mixture thickens.

SWEET & SOUR SPARERIBS
Tiem Shuen Pai Gut

Have your butcher cut 2 lbs. of ribs with a bandsaw in 1-1/2"
pieces. Add 2 cups of water or enough water to cover. Simmer
with a cover for 20 minutes. Remove pork and let cool.

Cup 1
1/4 cup wine vinegar
1/2 cup sugar
1/4 cup stock
1 tablespoon catsup
1-1/2 tablespoon corn starch
1/2 teaspoon salt
2 tablespoons pineapple syrup (from can)
1 tablespoons juice from sweet mixed pickles
1 tablespoon soy sauce

Plate 1
1/4 cup pineapple tidbits
1/4 cup sweet mixed pickles

Plate 2
2 tablespoons shredded coconut

Wok or pan, medium heat
1 tablespoon oil
1 teaspoon salt
2 cloves garlic minced fine

Add the ribs and brown them.
Add cup 1 and stir for 1 minute.
Then add plate 1 and stir until sauce thickens.
Add plate 2 for a garnish.

MOO SHI PORK

Plate 1

2 black mushrooms
2 tablespoons wood ears
These 2 ingredients should be soaked in warm water 30 minutes
and then cut in strips 1/8" wide.
15 dried golden needles, soaked in warm water 30 minutes,
hard tips removed and cut in half
2 scallions cut in 2" pieces then shredded
1/4 cup cabbage cut in 1/8" strips 2" long

Plate 2

2 eggs beaten. Heat a lightly oiled pan and cover bottom with a
thin layer of beaten egg. Fry until firm, then turn and fry the
other side. Repeat until eggs arc used up. Stack eggs in pile and
cut in strips 2"x1/8".

Mixing bowl

1 tablespoon dry sherry
1 tablespoon soy sauce
1 teaspoon corn starch
4 oz. uncooked pork cut in shreds 1/8"x1/8"x2"

Cup 1

1 teaspoon soy sauce
1 teaspoon dry sherry
1 teaspoon stock

Wok or pan, medium heat

2 tablespoons peanut oil

Add contents of mixing bowl to wok and stir fry 3 minutes until
pork changes to light brown.
Add plate 1 and stir fry 3 minutes.
Add cup 1 and cook with cover 2 minutes.
Add plate 2 and stir 1 minute.

This dish can be served with rice, but it is far better served with
pancakes. See the following recipe.

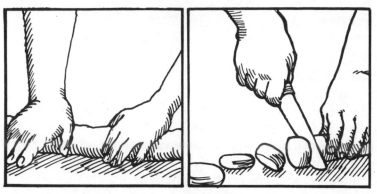

Roll dough in a rope 1-1/2" thick. Cut in 1/2" pieces.

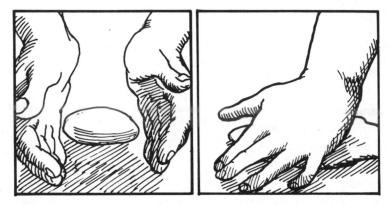

Roll or pat these pieces until they reach 3" diameter.

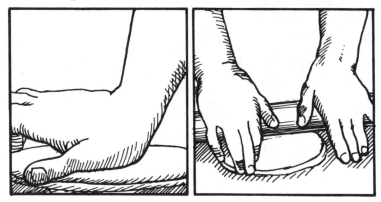

Stack pancakes in two's. Roll to 7" diameter.

ROLLING CHINESE PANCAKES

CHINESE PANCAKES
for Moo Shi Pork or Peking Duck

Place 2 cups sifted all purpose flour in a mixing bowl with 3/4 to 1 cup of boiling water. Add the boiling water slowly and stir with a chopstick until well mixed. When cool, knead with your hands for a few minutes. Then cover and refrigerate 15 minutes.

Roll the dough with your hands into a rope about 1-1/2" in diameter. Cut this into pieces 1/2" thick. Roll these pieces with a rolling pin until they form cakes about 3" in diameter.

Coat the top of the pancakes with peanut oil. Then stack the pancakes in two's. Roll again with a rolling pin on a floured board until a diameter of 7" is reached.

Heat a heavy frying pan to medium heat. Brush the pan with a very thin coating of oil. Place a 7" pancake in the pan. When the bottom begins to brown, repeat on the second side. When both sides are browned, remove from pan and separate the two halves.

Place 6 pancakes on aluminum foil and fold securely. Steam for 20 minutes. Or fold the pancakes in half, oil side in, and place on steamer tray. Cover with a clean towel and steam 10 minutes. The towel prevents the condensation from the cover from dripping on the pancakes.

To serve, place 1/4 teaspoon hoisin sauce on half the pancake. Place 2 tablespoons of filling on top of the hoisin sauce. Fold over to cover filling. Then fold bottom up to seal. Eat from the top.

PIGS FEET RED COOKED
Gee Gok See Yeow

Clean and split pigs feet. Add enough water to cover and simmer, covered, for 1 to 1-1/2 hours. Check and add more water if necessary during cooking period. Turn the feet every 20 minutes. Remove from pot. Place in colander and rinse. Clean the pot and replace the feet.

Add the following ingredients:

4 cups stock
4 tablespoons soy sauce
2 tablespoons dry sherry
2 slices ginger root minced fine
1/2 teaspoon salt

Bring to a boil and simmer, covered 2-1/4 hours. Add 1 teaspoon sugar. Simmer 15 minutes more until skin is tender and meat pulls away from the bones.

PORK WITH CELLOPHANE NOODLES
Gee Yoke Chow Fun See

Mixing bowl
8 oz. lean pork, cut in strips 1/8" thick, then in slices 1/8"x2"
2 tablespoons soy sauce
1/2 teaspoon sugar
Mix and allow the pork to marinate for a minimum of 15 minutes.

Plate 1
1/4 cup bamboo shoots, rinsed and cut 1/8"x2"
1/4 cup water chestnuts in 1/8"x2" strips
1/4 cup green pepper cut in 1/8"x2" strips
1/4 cup onion cut in 1/8" strips

Plate 2
4 oz. cellophane noodles (1 package), soaked in warm water 20
minutes, drained, then cut in 2" pieces

Cup 1
1/2 cup chicken stock

Wok or pan, medium heat
2 tablespoons peanut oil
1/2 teaspoon salt
1 clove garlic minced fine

When garlic is golden, add mixing bowl and stir until pork browns,
about 5 minutes.

Add plate 1 and stir fry 2 minutes.
Add plate 2 and stir fry 2 minutes.
Add cup 1 and cook, with cover, until gravy is absorbed, about
5 minutes.

QUICK STEWED PORK WITH CELLOPHANE NOODLES
Gee Yoke Chow Fun See

Plate 1
8 oz. raw pork cut in 3/4" cubes

Plate 2
4 oz. cellophane noodles (1 package)

Plate 3
4 oz. bamboo shoots, rinsed and drained, then cut in 1/4" cubes
4 oz. celery, sliced diagonally 1/4" thick
4 oz. canned mushrooms drained

Cup 1
1 cup chicken stock

Cup 2
1/2 cup chicken stock
1 tablespoon soy sauce
1 tablespoon dry sherry
1/2 teaspoon sugar

Wok or pan, medium heat
1 tablespoon peanut oil
1/2 teaspoon salt
1 clove garlic minced fine

When garlic is golden, add plate 1 and stir fry 3-5 minutes.

Add cup 1 and plate 2 and cook with cover for 5 minutes.
Add plate 3 and cook with cover for 5 minutes.
Add cup 2 and cook with cover for 5 minutes or until liquid is almost all gone.

Although this is not a real stew, it tastes somewhat like stew. The vegetables are steamed in the wok, and vegetables and meat reach their finished state at the same time.

ROAST PORK LO MEIN
Char Shu Lo Mein

Plate 1
4 oz. dried noodles. Drop in boiling water 10 minutes. Drain and rinse in cold water and drain again. Spread on platter to dry. When dry to the touch, toss in a mixing bowl with 1 tablespoon peanut oil until noodles are coated. This will make from 3/4 to 1 lb. of cooked noodles.
2 oz. bamboo shoots cut in 1/2" cubes. Rinse, then parboil 2 minutes.
2 oz. water chestnuts cut in slices 1/2" thick

Plate 2
4 oz. roast pork cut in 1/2" cubes
2 oz. lettuce in strips 1/2" wide

Cup 1
1 teaspoon dry sherry
3 tablespoons oyster sauce
1 teaspoon sugar
1/8 teaspoon sesame oil, optional
1 teaspoon soy sauce

Wok or pan, medium heat
1 tablespoon peanut oil
1/2 teaspoon salt
1 clove garlic minced fine
1 slice ginger 1/8" thick, minced fine

When garlic is golden, add plate 1 and stir 5 minutes.
Add plate 2 and stir 2 minutes.
Add cup 1 and stir 2 minutes.

ROAST PORK WITH BEAN SPROUTS
Gna Choy Chow Gee Yoke

Plate 1
1 lb. bean sprouts

Plate 2
4 oz. roast pork cut in strips 1/8"x3"

Cup 1
1/4 cup stock

Cup 2
1/4 cup stock
1/8 teaspoon sesame oil
1/2 teaspoon sugar
1 teaspoon dry sherry
1 teaspoon thick soy sauce
1 tablespoon corn starch
dash pepper

Wok or pan, medium heat
2 tablespoons oil
1/2 teaspoon salt
1 clove garlic, minced fine

Add plate 1 and stir fry 1 minute.
Add cup 1. Stir and then simmer with cover for 3 minutes.
Add plate 2 and stir fry 1 minute.
Add cup 2 and stir until it thickens slightly.
Add 1 scallion, white part only, cut in 1/4" pieces.

ROAST PORK WITH FRESH RICE NOODLES
Char Shu Sow How Fun

Plate 1
8 oz. fresh rice noodles cut in strips 1/2" wide and 6" long for easy handling
4 oz. roast pork cut in pieces 1/8"x1/2"x2"
4 oz. bean sprouts

Plate 2
2 scallions cut in 2" pieces, then in quarters

Cup 1
1 tablespoon oyster sauce
1 tablespoon soy sauce

Wok or pan, medium heat
1 tablespoon peanut oil
1 clove garlic minced fine

When garlic is golden, add plate 1 and stir fry 3 minutes.
Add plate 2 and stir fry 1 minute.
Add cup 1 and stir until noodles are coated.

BACON WITH CABBAGE & OYSTER SAUCE
Yee Choy Yen Yoke Ho Yo

Fry 4-6 slices of bacon until crisp. Remove from pan and drain the pan of all but 1 tablespoon bacon fat.
Add 1/2 teaspoon salt and 1 slice ginger minced fine to the fat.
Stir fry for 1 minute. Then add 2 cups of cabbage in 1"x2" pieces.
Stir until the cabbage is transparent, 1-2 minutes.
Add the cooked bacon and stir.
Add 1/4 cup of stock and cook with cover for 5 minutes.
Add 1 tablespoon oyster sauce and stir for 1 minute.

HAM FRIED RICE
For Tui Chow Fan

Plate 1
2 cups leftover white or brown rice. (Brown rice blends well in this dish, and the texture is interesting.)
2 oz. onion chopped the size of peas

Plate 2
4 oz. boiled ham cut 1/8"x1/4"x2"
1 oz. lettuce in strips 1/4"x2"
1 oz. water chestnuts sliced 1/8" thick
1 oz. bamboo shoots 1/8"x1/4"x2". Rinse & boil 2 minutes.
1 oz. green pepper 1/4"x2". If you want the pepper softer, boil it with the bamboo shoots.
1 egg scrambled in 1 teaspoon peanut oil in hot wok and rolled until it covers most of wok. Let set. Then roll up like jelly roll. Cut in strips 1/4" wide. Unroll and cut in 2" lengths.

Cup 1
1 tablespoon dry sherry
1 tablespoon soy sauce
1 tablespoon oyster sauce

Wok or pan, medium heat
2 tablespoons peanut oil
1/2 teaspoon salt
2 cloves garlic minced fine

When garlic is golden, add plate 1 and stir fry 5 minutes. Be sure to press out the lumps of rice so that the grains are separate.
Add plate 2 and stir fry 3 minutes.
Add cup 1 and stir until liquid is absorbed. This may take 2-3 minutes.

HAM & PINEAPPLE
For Tui Bo Lo

Plate 1
4 oz. bamboo shoots cut in 3/4" cubes. Rinse and parboil for 3 minutes.
8 water chestnuts. Leave whole if small. If larger than the bamboo shoots, cut in half.
6 black mushrooms. Soak in warm water 30 minutes. Remove stems and cut in halves or quarters to match the bamboo shoots.

Plate 2
8 oz. boiled ham cut in 3/4" cubes
8 oz. pineapple chunks
1/2 oz. seedless raisins

Cup 1
1/4 cup chicken stock
1/4 cup pineapple juice from the chunks
1 teaspoon soy sauce
1 teaspoon dry sherry

Cup 2
1/4 cup chicken stock
1 tablespoon corn starch

Wok or pan, medium heat
1 tablespoon peanut oil
1/2 teaspoon salt
1 clove garlic minced fine

When garlic is golden, add plate 1 and stir fry 5 minutes.
Add plate 2 and stir 1 minute.
Add cup 1 and cook with cover for 2 minutes.
Add cup 2 and stir until sauce thickens.

HAM & CHEESE TURNOVER

Plate 1
1 oz. boiled ham cut in 1/8"x1/8"x4" pieces
1 water chestnut minced in 1/8" pieces
1 slice onion 1/4" thick cut in half

Plate 2
1 slice cheddar cheese 1/4" thick by 1" by 4" cut in strips 1/8" wide

Cup 1
1 egg well beaten

Wok or pan, medium heat
1 teaspoon peanut oil

When oil starts to smoke, add plate 1. Stir 2 minutes.
Add 1 teaspoon soy sauce. Stir and return to plate 1.

Heat wok again and add 1 tablespoon peanut oil. When oil is hot, add cup 1 and roll around to cover bottom in a circle about 6-7" across. When egg starts to set, place everything from plate 1 on left side of circle of egg. Add plate 2 on top, then lift right side of egg over left side to cover. Add 1 teaspoon water to wok and cover for 1 minute. Uncover and turn over for other side. Egg should start to brown at this point. If not, heat can be turned up a little and egg given 1 or 2 more turns. Slide off to serving plate.

You may use 2 eggs if you wish. Other fillings can be used.
If you have a ring for the wok, when the right side of the egg is placed over the left, the wok can be tilted so that some of the egg in the center will run to the edge and help seal it. If you have a problem to form it, you can fold it like a spring roll in the pan, using the wok turner. The water helps to steam everything and makes it cook faster.

Lamb

Lamb is a regional specialty of northern China, Manchuria and Mangolia, which spread south into some of the other provinces, but never gained widespread popularity there. Lamb has a strong flavor and many Chinese from the south do not like it.

In this country, a few new Mandarin restaurants are serving lamb dishes, and you may expect more lamb on restaurant menus in the future, both in its original Manchurian style or modified into standard dishes like Lo Mein, Fried Rice, etc.

I buy lamb shoulder or leg. It is best to cut 2-4 steaks from the sirloin end of a leg of lamb, and save these for special dishes. The remainder of the leg can be boned and cut in 8 oz. portions. Similarly, the shoulder can be boned and cut in 8 oz. portions. Do not slice lamb any smaller than this—it will suffer from freezer burn. When you are ready, remove the 8 oz. lamb portion from the freezer and let thaw for a few minutes. Then slice when it is still firm. Any small pieces of lamb which are left over can be ground for lamb patties or combined with other chopped meat into meat loaf.

CHINESE ROAST LAMB
Shu Young Yoke

Lamb roasts nicely with Chinese seasonings.

3/4 cup soy sauce
2 cloves garlic
1/4 cup sugar
1 oz onion
2 tablespoons Del Monte catsup (made with pineapple vinegar)
1 slice lemon
1 slice ginger
2 tablespoons dry sherry

Blend the above 3 minutes at high speed.

Place a leg of lamb into a heavy plastic bag and add the marinade, above. Let remain in the refrigerator overnight, turning the lamb a few times to make sure it is covered with marinade.

Remove from bag and roast in the oven at 375 degrees until a meat thermometer gives an internal temperature of 165 degrees. While the leg is roasting, baste with marinade every 30 minutes.

Serve with steamed rice. If any lamb is left over, cut in 1" cubes and fry in lightly oiled wok until all sides are brown. Serve on a bed of lettuce. It provides a nice touch to mix 1 teaspoon salt and 1/2 teaspoon pepper and fry in a wok with no oil until light brown; place in a small heap on the side of the lamb or in a tiny salt dish— guests can dip the cubes of lamb in this fried salt and pepper.

LAMB WITH VEGETABLES
Qua Choy Chow Young Yoke

Plate 1
1 tablespoon soy sauce
1 tablespoon dry sherry
1 tablespoon peanut oil
8 oz. lean lamb cut in slices 1/16"x1/2"x1"
4 oz. bamboo shoots, rinsed and drained, sliced 1/16"x1/2"x1"
4 oz. water chestnuts sliced 1/16"
4 oz. canned mushrooms, stems and pieces
Stir and let lamb and vegetables marinate at least 15 minutes.

Plate 2
6 scallions cut in 1" pieces

Cup 1
1 tablespoon soy sauce
1 tablespoon dry sherry
1 tablespoon wine vinegar
2 tablespoons chicken stock
1/2 teaspoon sesame seed oil, optional

Cup 2
1/4 cup chicken stock
1 tablespoon corn starch

Wok or pan, highest heat
1 tablespoon peanut oil
1 clove garlic minced fine

When garlic is golden, add plate 1 and stir till lamb is brown, 2-4 minutes depending on your stove.
Add plate 2 and stir 1 minute.
Add cup 1 and cook with cover for 1 minute.
Add cup 2 and stir until sauce thickens.
In this dish the marinade of plate 1 is placed in the wok along with the lamb and the vegetables.

LAMB WITH SCALLIONS
Gow Choy Chow Young Yoke

Plate 1
1 tablespoon soy sauce
1 tablespoon dry sherry
1 tablespoon peanut oil
8 oz. lean lamb sliced 1/16"x1/2"x1"

Mix and let marinate at least 15 minutes.

Plate 2
6 scallions cut in 1" pieces

Cup 1
1 tablespoon soy sauce
1 tablespoon dry sherry
1 teaspoon wine vinegar
1/2 teaspoon sesame oil, optional
plus the marinade left over in plate 1 after lamb is added to wok.

Wok or pan, highest heat
1 tablespoon peanut oil
1 clove garlic minced fine

When garlic is golden, add lamb only to wok, not the marinade, and pour left over marinade into cup 1.
Stir rapidly until lamb is brown, 2-4 minutes.
Add plate 2 and stir 1 minute.
Add cup 1 and stir 1 minute.

CURRIED LAMB
Gar Lee Young Yoke

Plate 1
1 lb. lean lamb cut in 1" cubes

Plate 2
4 oz. potato cut in 1" cubes
4 oz. carrots cut in 1/2" slices

Plate 3
4 oz. canned mushrooms, stems and pieces
2 oz. water chestnuts sliced 1/4" thick
1 small green pepper cut in 1" pieces

Cup 1
2 teaspoons curry powder
1 cup chicken stock

Pan or wok, medium heat
1 tablespoon peanut oil
1/4 teaspoon salt
1 clove garlic minced fine
1 slice ginger, 1/8" thick, minced fine

When garlic is golden, add plate 1 and stir until meat browns, about 4 minutes.
Add plate 2 and stir 2 minutes.
Add cup 1 and cook with cover 20 minutes. Check to make sure liquid has not evaporated. If it has, add 1/2 cup water.
Add plate 3 and cook with cover 5 minutes.
If you wish a thicker gravy, add 1/2 cup stock and 1 teaspoon corn starch, and stir until mixture thickens.

Seafood

If you live on the seaboard, buying fresh seafood is no problem—just go to your neighborhood fish store. If you live within 300 miles of the coast, fresh fish is generally brought in by truck once a week, usually on Wednesday, so that people can buy fish ahead of time for Friday. Plan your fish meals for Wednesday when the fish will be at its peak of freshness.

When you buy fillets, cut them in 4 oz. portions and freeze flat in a tray in your freezer. If you buy a whole fish, clean it inside and out, and freeze the whole thing. You can take the head off or leave it on, Chinese style. When you are ready to proceed with any recipe, remove the fish from the freezer, wait 10 minutes and slice as thinly as you wish.

Look for a wonderful new fish imported frozen from China and available in Chinese grocery stores—yellow fish, especially good in sweet and sour dishes.

If you live inland, buy shrimp in 5 lb. blocks, frozen. They can be separated in ice water and used. The remaining block can be placed back in the freezer.

You can buy shrimp in a variety of sizes, going from the largest and most expensive to the smallest and least expensive. Use the large shrimp for stir fry dishes, where appearance counts for a great deal. Use the smaller shrimp for soups, egg rolls, dim sums, and fried rice.

If you can't get fresh lobster, try frozen lobster tails. These are both tasty and cheap. They come from lobsters with small front claws—there is so little meat in these, the producers don't bother shipping the entire lobster to market.

STEAMED TURBOT ON RICE
Jing Yu Fan

1 lb. turbot cut in 1"x2" pieces
1 slice ginger 1/4" thick, minced fine
1 tablespoon soy sauce
1 tablespoon dry sherry
Stir and marinate at least 30 minutes.
Prepare rice by any method in Rice Chapter. After 5 minutes of cooking, place fish on top of rice, put the cover back on the pot, and continue cooking for 25 minutes.

STEAMED SEA BASS WITH BLACK BEANS ON RICE
Jing Yu Dow See Fan

1 lb. sea bass fillet cut in 1/2"x2" strips
1 slice ginger 1/4" thick minced fine
1/2 teaspoon black beans, washed and minced
1 tablespoon soy sauce
1 tablespoon dry sherry

Stir and let marinate for at least 30 minutes.
Follow rice directions as above. After 30 minutes, turn off heat and add 1 scallion cut in matchstick strips. Let stand 2 minutes covered.

STEAMED FLOUNDER WITH MUSHROOMS ON RICE
Jing Yu Moo Goo Fan

1 lb. flounder fillet cut in 1" squares
4 black mushrooms soaked and cut in pieces 1/2"x1"
1 slice ginger 1/4" thick minced fine
1 clove garlic minced fine
1 tablespoon soy sauce
1 tablespoon dry sherry
1/2 teaspoon sugar

Stir and marinate for 30 minutes. Follow directions as above.
You can use any mild flavored fish for these three recipes.

Seafood/175

HADDOCK IN BLACK BEANS
Dow See Yu

Plate 1
4 oz. onion cut in thin strips
1 stalk celery cut in thin slices

Plate 2
8 oz. haddock fillet, whole

Cup 1
1 teaspoon soy sauce
1 tablespoon dry sherry
1/2 cup chicken stock

Wok or pan, medium heat
1 tablespoon peanut oil
1 clove garlic minced fine
1 slice ginger 1/4" thick, minced fine
1 teaspoon black beans, washed and minced

Stir until garlic turns golden.
Add plate 1 and stir 2-3 minutes.
Push everything away to corners of pan to make room for fish.
Add plate 2 and let heat for 3 minutes on each side. Then add
cup 1 and cook with cover 3 minutes on each side. Remove
fish to plate and pour sauce over the fish.

This dish has a dark color and is not usually served—most people
are hesitant to try black beans. The flavor of this dish is
wonderful, due to the black beans and the garlic. Try it.

TROUT ON CARROT WAVES

Plate 1
2 trout about 7-8" long, cleaned without heads

Plate 2
1 oz. bamboo shoots cut in thin strips with potato peeler
1 oz. water chestnuts sliced 1/16" thick
2 oz. carrots cut in strips with potato peeler

Cup 1
1 tablespoon soy sauce
1 tablespoon dry sherry

Wok or pan, medium heat
1 tablespoon butter or margerine
1 clove garlic minced fine
1 slice ginger 1/8" thick, minced fine

When garlic is golden, lower heat and add plate 1.
Turn trout every few minutes until fish turns white. Keep wok covered while cooking.
Add plate 2 and cup 1 and cook with cover for 3 minutes.

Two scallions may be cut in 2" pieces and placed in the body cavity of the trout. The scallions steam during the cooking process. The color of the scallions is a nice contrast to the other vegetables.

When you serve this dish, place the trout on top of the vegetables, like fish riding the waves. Scoop some vegetables towards the front of the fish, where the heads would be.

SWEET & SOUR FISH, WHOLE
Tiem Shuen Yu

Take a 1 to 1-1/2 lb. sea bass, carp, porgy, or similar fish. Clean and scale. Remove fins and gills. Chinese people prefer to leave the head on. You can remove it if you like. Make a few slashes on an angle about 1/4" deep on both sides of fish. Dry with a paper towel. Then coat both sides of fish with beaten egg and roll in corn starch which has been spread on wax paper. You can lift the paper up to help make the corn starch stick to the fish. Turn the fish over to coat the other side with corn starch. Some people prefer to coat the fish with egg once more and then roll in corn starch once more, but this procedure is optional.

Heat oil to 350 degrees and cook fish until golden brown. If you use a wok, have about 1" of oil between the fish and the sides of the wok, which for a 1 lb. fish is 1 quart of oil. For a 1-1/2 lb. fish, use 1 more cup of oil. Drain on a paper towel. Remove towel and place on serving dish and keep warm.

Plate 1
1 green pepper cut in strips, about 4 oz.
3 slices pineapple cut in thin strips
2 oz. onion cut in strips

Cup 1
1/4 cup wine vinegar
1/2 cup sugar
1/4 cup chicken stock
1 tablespoon catsup
1-1/2 tablespoon corn starch
2 tablespoons syrup from pineapple
1 tablespoon soy sauce

Wok or pan, medium heat
1 tablespoon oil

Add plate 1 and simmer with cover 2-3 minutes.
Add cup 1 and simmer until mixture thickens.
Pour over fish which has been kept warm on platter.

SWEET & SOUR FISH SLICES
Tiem Shuen Yu Pen

Take a lb. halibut or haddock fillet and cut it in 1"x2" strips.
Dredge with flour. Make a batter of

1/4 cup flour, all purpose
1/4 cup corn starch
1 egg
1/4 teaspoon salt
1 tablespoon or a little more if needed of water

Dip fish strips in batter and deep fry at 375 degrees until golden.
Remove to paper towel to drain. Place on serving dish and keep
warm in oven.

Plate 1
1/4 cup pineapple tidbits
1/4 cup sweet mixed pickles
2 oz. carrot peeled in thin strips with potato peeler

Cup 1
1/4 cup wine vinegar
1/2 cup sugar
1/4 cup stock
1 tablespoon catsup
1-1/2 tablespoons corn starch
1/2 teaspoon salt
2 tablespoons syrup from pineapple
1 tablespoon soy sauce

Wok or pan, medium heat
1 tablespoon peanut oil
1 clove garlic minced fine
1 slice ginger minced fine

When garlic is golden, add plate 1 and stir fry 2 minutes.
Add cup 1 and stir until mixture thickens.
Pour mixture in wok over fish which has been kept warm.

The color combination here is unusual. It is worthy of being
a featured dish and the cost is low.

FRIED YELLOW FISH

Formerly impossible to import, this fish is now becoming common in Chinese grocery stores and restaurants. The fish tastes wonderful, but has a nasty looking set of teeth. The first time the fish was served to me, it was standing on its belly with its mouth open a bit. The waiter placed the platter on the table and then waited for me to react. I was initially shocked, but the beauty of the dish set me at ease. A companion later explained that it was an honor to be presented with the fish facing me.

Take a fish, about 1-1/2 lbs., and thaw. Rinse in cold water, drain, and cut 3-4 diagonal gashes on each side of the fish, 1/4" deep. Dust fish with corn starch. I use a small flour sifter to dust the fish with starch. The coating should not be thick.

Pour 1" peanut oil in wok. Heat to 325 degrees. Lower fish in oil and fry 4-5 minutes each side. Turn for a second frying on each side. Total frying time should be 12-15 minutes. When done, the fins should be crispy and almost fall apart. Remove to a heated plate. If the fish is too big for your pan it can be cut in half and then put together on the serving plate.

Remove all but 1 tablespoon oil from wok. Reduce heat to medium. Add
1/4 teaspoon salt
1 clove garlic minced fine
1 slice ginger minced fine

When garlic is golden, add
4 oz. canned mushrooms, stems and pieces
6 oz. bean sprouts
2 oz. water chestnuts sliced 1/8" thick
2 oz. bamboo shoots, drained & rinsed, cut in matchsticks

Stir fry 3 minutes. Then add
1 tablespoon soy sauce
1 tablespoon dry sherry
1/4 cup chicken stock

Turn heat to high and stir 2-3 minutes. When liquid is down to 1/4 cup, place the vegetables on top of the fish on the platter and serve with rice.

SHRIMPS WITH CUCUMBER
Wong Gar Chow Har

Plate 1
8 oz. shrimp, shelled and deveined, dried with paper towel
to prevent oil spatter

Plate 2
8 oz. cucumber. Peel strips lengthwise with potato peeler to
make green and white stripes. Cut in half lengthwise. Use a
teaspoon to remove seeds. Cut slices 1/8" thick.

Cup 1
1/4 cup chicken stock
1 tablespoon sherry
1/2 teaspoon soy sauce

Cup 2
1/4 cup soy sauce
1 tablespoon corn starch

Wok or pan, medium heat
1 tablespoon peanut oil
1 clove garlic minced fine

When garlic is golden, add plate 1 and stir until shrimp turns
white, about 2-3 minutes. Return shrimp to plate 1.
Add 1 more tablespoon of oil to wok and heat. When oil
bubbles at edges, add plate 2 and stir fry 3 minutes until
cucumbers are opaque.
Return plate 1 to wok.
Add cup 1 and cook with cover for 2 minutes until sauce boils.
Add cup 2 and stir until sauce thickens.

SHRIMPS WITH BEAN SPROUTS
Gna Choy Har

Plate 1
1/2 lb. shrimp cleaned
4 pieces wood ears, soaked in warm water 15 minutes, rinsed,
hard stems removed

Plate 2
1 lb. bean sprouts

Cup 1
1/3 cup stock, chicken or pork
1/4 teaspoon sugar

Cup 2
1 tablespoon thick soy sauce
1 tablespoon corn starch
dash pepper
1/4 cup stock of any kind.

Wok or pan, medium heat
1 tablespoon oil
1/2 teaspoon salt
1 clove garlic minced

Heat until garlic is golden. Add plate 1 and stir fry 1 minute.
Add 1 teaspoon dry sherry. Stir fry 1 minute.
Add plate 2 and stir.
Add cup 1 and cook with cover 3 minutes.
Add cup 2 and cook until mixture thickens.
Add 1 scallion, white part, cut in 1/4" pieces.

SHRIMPS WITH PEAS
Ching Dau Chow Har

Plate 1
8 oz. shrimp, shelled and deveined, dried on paper towels

Plate 2
8 oz. frozen peas or fresh peas

Cup 1
3/4 cup chicken stock
1/2 teaspoon sugar
1 tablespoon soy sauce
1 tablespoon dry sherry

Cup 2
1/4 cup chicken stock
1 tablespoon corn starch

Cup 3, Optional
1 scallion cut in 1/4" slices

Wok or pan, medium heat
2 tablespoons peanut oil
1 clove garlic minced fine
1 slice ginger 1/4" thick minced fine

When garlic is golden, add plate 1 and stir fry 1 minute.
Add cup 1. When liquid boils, cover and simmer 2 minutes.
Add plate 2 and simmer with cover for 2 minutes.
Add cup 2 and stir until sauce thickens.
Add cup 3 if desired.

SHRIMP WITH VEGETABLES
Chow Har Kow

Clean and devein 1/2 lb. shrimp. Dry with paper towel and dip in the following batter:

1 egg lightly beaten
1/2 cup all purpose flour
1 tablespoon cold water
1/2 teaspoon salt

Heat about 2"-3" of peanut oil to 375 degrees and deep fry the shrimp for about 8 minutes until golden brown. Put aside until needed.

Plate 1
1 oz. canned or fresh mushrooms
1 oz. snow peas
4 oz. bok choy in 1" pieces
1 oz. bamboo shoots cut in matchsticks
2 water chestnuts in 1/8" slices

Cup 1
7/8 cup chicken stock
1/2 teaspoon sugar
1 tablespoon dry sherry

Cup 2
1 tablespoon corn starch
1 teaspoon thick soy sauce
2 tablespoons stock
1/4 teaspoon sesame oil

Wok or pan, medium heat
1 tablespoon oil
1/2 teaspoon salt
2 minced garlic cloves

Heat until garlic turns golden. Add plate 1 and stir 30 seconds. Add cup 1 and cook with cover 5 minutes.

Add cup 2 and stir 1 minute until mixture thickens.
Add the shrimp, turn off heat, and stir 2 minutes.
184/Seafood

HOT SHRIMP WITH VEGETABLES

Plate 1
8 oz. shrimp. Shell and devein.

Plate 2
4 oz. bamboo shoots, rinsed and cut 1"x1/4"x1/4"
4 oz. water chestnuts cut 1/4"x1/4"x1"
4 oz. cabbage in strips 1/4"x1"
2 scallions in 1" pieces
4 oz. canned mushrooms, stems and pieces

Cup 1
1/2 cup chicken stock
1/2 teaspoon sugar
1 teaspoon soy sauce
1 tablespoon hoisin sauce
1 teaspoon Tabasco or hot pepper sauce
1 tablespoon catsup

Cup 2
1/4 cup chicken stock
1 tablespoon corn starch

Wok or pan, medium heat
1 tablespoon peanut oil
1 clove garlic minced fine
1 slice ginger 1/8" thick, minced fine

When garlic is golden, add plate 1 and stir fry 2 minutes. Return shrimp to plate 1.
If wok needs more oil, add 1 tablespoon more. When hot, add 1/2 teaspoon salt.
Add plate 2 and stir fry 3 minutes.

Add cup 1 and cook with cover 3 minutes after liquid bubbles.
Add plate 1 and cook with cover 3 minutes.
Uncover and add cup 2. Stir until sauce thickens.

SHRIMPS IN LOBSTER SAUCE
Dow See Har

Plate 1
4 oz. ground pork or beef

Plate 2
1 lb. shrimp, cleaned and deveined

Plate 3
2 eggs beaten lightly

Cup 1
1-3/4 cup chicken stock

Cup 2
4 tablespoons chicken stock
2-1/2 tablespoons corn starch

Cup 3
1 tablespoon soy sauce
1/4 teaspoon sesame oil, optional
1/2 teaspoon sugar
1/2 teaspoon salt

Cup 4
1 scallion cut in 1/4" pieces, white part only

Wok or pan, medium heat
2 tablespoons peanut oil
2 cloves garlic minced fine
1 teaspoon black beans, washed and minced

Heat until garlic is golden. Then add plate 1. Break meat into very small pieces until it is all brown.
Add plate 2 and stir fry 1 minute.
Add 1 tablespoon dry sherry, stir and cook, covered, 2 minutes.
Add cup 1, cover, and simmer 3 minutes.
Add cup 2, turn heat down to low, and stir.
Add plate 3 and stir until egg breaks into strands.
Add cup 3 and stir for a few seconds.
Add cup 4 and stir. Turn off heat and let stand for 1 minute.

CURRIED SHRIMP
Gar Lee Chor Har

Plate 1
8 oz. shrimp, shelled and deveined

Plate 2
2 oz. onion, wedge cut
4 oz. canned mushrooms
4 oz. frozen peas

Cup 1
1 teaspoon soy sauce
1 teaspoon dry sherry

Cup 2
1/2 cup chicken stock
2 teaspoons curry powder

Cup 3
1 tablespoon corn starch
1/4 cup chicken stock

Wok or pan, medium heat
1 tablespoon peanut oil
1 clove garlic minced fine
1 slice ginger root 1/8" thick, minced fine

When garlic is golden, add plate 1 and stir fry 2 minutes.
Add cup 1 and stir 1 minute. Return shrimp to plate 1.
Add 1 tablespoon oil to wok and heat.
Add plate 2 and stir 2 minutes.
Add cup 2 and stir until mixture simmers. Cover and simmer
for 3 minutes.
Add cup 3 and stir until sauce thickens.
Add plate 1 and stir 30 seconds.

This dish was new to me until I went to England. It is simple to
prepare and unusual to Americans. You may wish to increase the
amount of curry, or you may wish to soften the flavor by adding
1 tablespoon catsup to cup 3.

HOT PEKING SHRIMP

Plate 1
8 oz. shrimp. Shell and devein. Dry on paper towel.

Plate 2
6 scallions cut in pieces 1" long

Cup 1
1/2 cup chicken stock
1/2 teaspoon sugar
1 teaspoon soy sauce
1 tablespoon hoisin sauce
1 teaspoon Tabasco sauce or hot pepper sauce. Add more if you like.

Wok or pan, medium heat
1 tablespoon peanut oil
1 clove garlic minced fine
1 slice ginger root 1/8" thick, minced fine

When garlic is golden, add plate 1 and stir fry 2 minutes.
Add plate 2 and stir fry 2 minutes.
Add cup 1 and when liquid starts to bubble, cover and simmer for 3 minutes.

STEAMED LOBSTER
Jeng Loong Har

Take a 1-1/4 lb. lobster, clean it, and cut it into 1" pieces.
Leave the shell on, but crack the claws.

Place in a mixing bowl:

8 oz. chopped meat (beef, pork, or chicken)
1 egg slightly beaten
1 clove garlic minced
1/2 teaspoon sugar
1/2 teaspoon salt
dash pepper
1/2 teaspoon sesame oil
1 tablespoon black beans, mashed

Mix thoroughly and spoon over lobster which has been placed
in a Pyrex baking dish.

Heat 1 tablespoon sesame oil and 1 tablespoon soy sauce and
pour over lobster. Place baking dish on a trivet in a large pot
with boiling water 1/2" below dish. Cover pot and steam for
15 minutes. Add 2 scallions, in 1/2" pieces, and steam 2 minutes
more. If you wish a slightly different texture, wait and add the
hot sesame oil and soy sauce in the final cooking period when
you add the scallions.

A Lobster Story—The best time to check out a new Chinese restaurant is after the lunch crowd leaves, when the chef and the waiters eat lunch in the dining room. Then, if you show that you have some knowledge of and interest in Chinese cooking, you can pick up many new recipes and interesting stories. One time I came into a restaurant about 2:30 in the afternoon. The waitress had gone shopping and the chef came out to take my order. I ordered Lobster Cantonese, one of my favorite dishes. When he brought me the dish, I requested chopsticks. He watched me eat for a while—he was making won tons—and then came over to talk. He had an interesting story to tell.

A customer once complained about waiting too long for steamed lobster, which takes 5 minutes preparation time and 15 minutes steaming time. Not wanting to lose the customer, the chef experimented, using the same ingredients but different techniques. When he stir fried the lobster, he obtained the best results. The customer was happy and a great new dish was born.

LOBSTER CANTONESE
Dow See Lung Har

Take a live 1-1/2 lb. lobster. Put it in water which is at room temperature for 30 minutes. This will put the lobster to sleep. Split the lobster down the belly from head to tail. Cut the tail off, and then in half. Cut off the small claws and the large claws. Crack the large claws by hitting them with the flat edge of a cleaver. Remove top of head shell. Remove green liver and orange coral—save for use on toast or in soup. Clean out the stomach completely and split the remaining shell in half across. Place it on plate 1.

Plate 1
Lobster from above
4 oz. ground pork or beef

Plate 2
2 eggs beaten slightly

Cup 1
1-3/4 cup chicken stock

Cup 2
2-1/2 tablespoons corn starch
4 tablespoons chicken stock

Cup 3
1 teaspoon soy sauce
1/4 teaspoon sesame oil, optional
1/2 teaspoon sugar
1/2 teaspoon salt

Cup 4
1 scallion cut in 1/4" pieces

Wok or pan, medium heat
2 tablespoons peanut oil
2 cloves garlic minced fine
1 teaspoon black beans, minced

When garlic is golden, add plate 1 until meat is light brown.
Add the lobster and stir 2 minutes until shell starts to turn red.
Add 1 tablespoon dry sherry and stir 1 minute. Turn heat to high.
Add cup 1 and boil with cover 3 minutes. Turn heat down.
Add cup 2 and stir until sauce thickens.
Add plate 2 and stir until   eggs break into shreds, 2-3 seconds.
Add cup 3 and stir 3 seconds.
Add cup 4. Stir and serve.

LOBSTER SOONG

Take a live 1-1/2 lb. lobster and place it in water which is at room temperature. This will put it to sleep. Split the lobster down the belly from head to tail. Cut off the tail and then cut the tail in half. Cut off the small claws. Cut off the large claws and crack by hitting with flat of cleaver. Remove top of head shell. Remove green liver and orange coral and save for use on toast or in soup. Clean out everything connected to stomach and split remaining shell in half crosswise.

Split a 4 oz. package of bean thread in 4 portions. Heat 1 quart of peanut oil to 375 degrees. Drop a single portion of bean thread into the oil. It should puff up within 2 seconds. Turn with a spatula for 1 second and then remove to colander to drain. Make a second portion in the same way. Place the other 2 portions remaining in a plastic container with cover and keep for future use.

Plate 1
4 oz. ground pork or beef
4 black mushrooms soaked and cut in quarters
2 oz. water chestnuts sliced 1/4" thick
2 oz. bamboo shoots, rinsed and cut 1/4"x1/4"x2"
2 oz. frozen or fresh peas

Plate 2
2 eggs lightly beaten with chopstick

Cup 1
1-3/4 cup chicken stock

Cup 2
2-1/2 tablespoons corn starch
4 tablespoons chicken stock

Cup 3
1 teaspoon soy sauce
1/4 teaspoon sesame oil, optional
1/2 teaspoon sugar
1/2 teaspoon salt

Cup 4
1 scallion cut in 1/4" pieces

Wok or pan, medium heat
2 tablespoons peanut oil
2 cloves garlic minced fine
1 teaspoon black beans, minced

When garlic turns golden, add plate 1 and stir until meat browns.
Add the lobster and stir 2 minutes until shell turns red.
Add 1 tablespoon dry sherry and stir 1 minute. Turn heat high.
Add cup 1 and boil with cover for 3 minutes.
Turn heat down and add cup 2. Stir until sauce thickens.
Add plate 2 and stir until eggs break into shreds, 2-3 seconds.
Add cup 3 and stir 3 seconds.
Add cup 4, stir and turn heat off.
Pour into a serving dish and top with bean thread (noodles)
which you have fried and placed in colander.

This dish is almost the same as Lobster Cantonese, but the extra
vegetables and noodles make the finished product very different.
If you prefer, the dish can be converted to Shrimp Soong—simply
substitute 1 lb. of shrimp (shelled and deveined) for the lobster.

STIR FRIED LOBSTER WITH BEAN SPROUTS
Chow Loong Har Gna Choy

Take 8 oz. lobster tails and thaw in refrigerator.
Drop in boiling water 1 minute. When cool, remove shell and cut
in pieces 1/2" thick.

Plate 1
1 lb. bean sprouts
1 oz. canned mushrooms

Plate 2
3 scallions cut in pieces 2" long

Cup 1
1/2 cup chicken stock

Cup 2
1/4 cup stock
1 tablespoon corn starch

Wok or pan, medium heat
1 tablespoon peanut oil
1/4 teaspoon salt
1 clove garlic minced fine

When garlic turns golden, add the lobster tails and stir fry
1 minute.
Add plate 1 and stir 1 minute.
Add cup 1 and cook with cover 2 minutes.
Add cup 2 and stir until sauce thickens.

Desserts

Desserts are not absolutely essential in Chinese meals, because by the time you get through with appetizers, soup, and main dishes, you are pretty full. When they are served, they range from simple to very elaborate. I myself prefer simple desserts, fruit or gelatin or almond cookies. If you wish, you can buy fortune cookies at a grocery store—they add humor and fun to any meal.

HONEY APPLES
But See Ping Quo

At first glance, this recipe may look too messy to try. However, if you once try these, you will not care about the work.

Peel 3 apples, core them, and then cut them in 6-8 wedges. There is a stainless steel tool which can core and cut in wedges in one operation. Drop apples in a solution of 1 quart water, 1 teaspoon salt, and 1 teaspoon lemon juice, in order to prevent them from from turning color while you do the other preparations.

Mixing bowl
2 tablespoons corn starch
3 tablespoons all purpose flour
2 egg whites
Mix together until smooth. Drain apples and place in mixing bowl and toss so that the batter covers all the wedges.

Wok or pan, medium heat
Heat 2-3 cups oil to 375 degrees. Lift apples from batter with chopsticks and deep fry them until golden in color. Remove from pan and drain in colander.

Use another wok or frying pan and heat to medium:
1 cup honey
1/2 cup sugar
1/4 cup water
When mixture thickens, test with one chopstick—dip the chopstick into the sugar mixture and then in ice water. When ready, the mixture should form a thread or teardrop on the end of the chopstick. Turn off heat and add 1 teaspoon sesame seeds. Then add apples and stir until all are coated. Bring pan to table. Using a pair of chopsticks, lift each apple from pan and dip it into a bowl of water with 1 tray of ice cubes in it. The coating will quickly harden, 5-8 seconds, and then the apples may be served to your guests.

BANANAS IN HONEY
But See Heung Jiu

This is easier to prepare than Honey Apples, but equally good.

Use firm yellow bananas. Cut them in half lengthwise.
Heat 2 tablespoons peanut oil in wok or pan at medium heat.
Lightly brown bananas on both sides. Then cut them in pieces
1" long.

Place in a wok or pan
1 cup honey
1/2 cup brown sugar
1/4 cup water
1 teaspoon either cider or wine vinegar

Heat until mixture starts to thicken. Use low setting. Check
with a chopstick until mixture forms a thread or tear drop when
dipped into cold water.add bananas to mixture of sugar and
honey and gently stir to make sure they are coated completely.

Bring pan to table and, using chopsticks, dip each piece of fruit
into a bowl of ice and water.The coating sets in 5-8 seconds.

ALMOND FRUIT GELATIN

This is a simple dessert which can be changed to your taste. A
basic topping is given, but other fruits such as mandarin oranges,
lichee nuts, or cherries, can be substituted.

Cup 1
1/3 cup water
1 envelope unflavored gelatin
Mix and let stand.

Place 1-1/2 cups of milk in a saucepan. Bring it to a boil.
Add 1/3 cup sugar. Stir then add cup 1 and stir.
Add 1 teaspoon almond extract. Stir and then pour into a
glass dish 8" in diameter and refrigerate until set. When set, 4-6
hours, cut into strips 1" wide in one direction. Then cut strips
at right angles to the first strips. This will give 1" squares.
Separate into 6 bowls and top with fruit cocktail and syrup.
198/Desserts

CHINESE SPONGE CAKE
Gai Don Go

4 eggs
1 cup sugar
1/4 teaspoon baking powder
1 cup flour
1 teaspoon vanilla

Beat 4 eggs until stiff. Some people separate whites and yolks, but if you have a good electric beater, the separation is not necessary. Add the sugar slowly a tablespoon at a time. Add the baking powder and flour (all purpose) together. Add the vanilla. Then continue beating a few minutes.

Grease a round 8"x8" pan. You can line this with wax paper or greased brown paper if you like.
Steam the cake in a steamer for 20 minutes. Check with a toothpick. If it does not come out clean, steam the cake for another 5 minutes.
Fry 1 tablespoon sesame seeds in a dry pan (not oiled) until golden and sprinkle on top of sponge cake.Cut in squares and serve. You can make cupcakes if you like by pouring batter into cup cake papers and steam for 15 minutes. Top with sesame seeds.

ALMOND COOKIES

2 cups all purpose flour
1/4 teaspoon salt
1 cup sugar
1 teaspoon baking powder
1 cup butter or lard or shortening
1 egg well beaten
1 teaspoon almond extract

Place everything in a mixing bowl and stir at low speed (electric beater) until uniform in color. If you don't have an electric beater, use your hands. Cover and refrigerate for 30 minutes to 1 hour for greater ease in handling.

Roll into balls 1" in diameter and place on greased cookie sheet 1" apart. Press a blanched almond into the center of each cookie. Bake in preheated oven at 350 degrees for 15-20 minutes until edges of cookies are light golden brown.
Yield: 36 cookies

*Quantity
Cooking*

Chinese luncheons or suppers are very popular at our church. Not only is the food simple to prepare—it is very economical, and the margin of profit is high. Moreover, Chinese cuisine is a welcome change from the usual turkey and ham meals offered to the public.

Because most churches do not own restaurant equipment, the recipes I give here are geared for limited or home equipment. To make up a menu for 25, choose 1 soup, 1 appetizer, boiled rice, 1 or 2 main courses depending on the appetite of the people you are serving, tea, and a simple dessert. You may prefer to buy almond cookies from a Chinese grocery store.

For service of the main items, I recommend buying paper plates with three compartments—serve the egg roll in one compartment, the rice in the second, and the main dish in the third. The combination will look very good.

Here is a sample menu for 25 people:

egg drop soup
boiled rice
pepper steak and/or chicken with mushrooms
tea
almond fruit gelatin or almond cookies

For 50 people add another main dish—sweet & sour meatballs are good—and double the other dishes.

BOILED RICE FOR 25 PEOPLE

Place 8-1/2 cups uncooked white rice in a large heavy pot with a tight fitting cover. Add water to cover the rice, until the point where the water touches the joint of the thumb while the thumb is touching the top of the rice.

Bring the pot to a boil rapidly. Then turn the heat down and simmer the rice for 30 minutes with the cover on. The rice can remain on simmer for 1 hour as long as there is some water left at the bottom of the pot.
1/3 cup of raw rice makes about 1 cup of cooked rice.
If rice is left over, it can be reheated by adding about 1/2 cup of water and setting the heat on low until water disappears from bottom of pot. The rice will steam to correct temperature within 10-15 minutes.

CHICKEN CORN SOUP FOR 25 PEOPLE

Place 6 quarts of water and 1 lb. raw boned chicken minced fine into a 12 quart pot, stainless steel if possible. Bring to a boil and simmer 10 minutes.

Add 4 oz. Virginia ham or any smoked ham minced fine along with a 6-1/2 lb. can, commercial size, of creamed corn. Bring to a boil and then add 6 eggs stirred lightly. Mix with chopstick to break up the eggs into shreds.

Add 1/4 cup dry sherry.
This soup is simple but the finished product is quite elegant.
The taste is unusual—the combination of creamed corn, chicken, and smoked ham works perfectly.
I fugured each serving as 8 oz. There will be enough extra soup for a few seconds (about 5-8 portions) which I am sure will be requested along with the recipe.

BASIC EGG DROP SOUP FOR 25 PEOPLE

Use a 12 quart pot, stainless steel if possible. Place in pot

16 envelopes MBT Chicken Bouillon or 16 chicken bouillon cubes
1 cup corn starch
2 teaspoons salt
1/4 teaspoon sesame or peanut oil
2 teaspoons soy sauce
6 oz. onion minced fine
8 quarts water

Stir to dissolve corn starch and bring to a boil.
Add 8 eggs, beaten lightly, from a pitcher with a pouring lip, and break the stream of egg with a fork or chopstick as egg hits the surface of the soup. This will break the eggs into shreds. Cover and simmer until needed.

CHICKEN EGG DROP SOUP FOR 25 PEOPLE

Add 1 cup raw boned chicken minced fine when you add the water. Directions remain the same.

MUSHROOM EGG DROP SOUP FOR 25 PEOPLE

Add 8 oz. canned or fresh mushrooms sliced 1/8" thick when you add the chicken before soup boils. Directions remain the same.

TOMATO EGG DROP SOUP FOR 25 PEOPLE

Add 4 cups fresh chopped tomatoes to the Chicken Egg Drop Soup before soup boils. No mushrooms in this recipe.

Although these recipes are for 25 people, I have figured some extra soup in order to take care of requests for seconds.

CHICKEN CHOP SUEY OR CHICKEN CHOW MEIN FOR 25 PEOPLE

Take 6 lb. raw boned chicken and slice it 1/4"x1/4"x2".
Fry about 3/4 of a lb. at a time in 1 tablespoon peanut oil
until chicken turns white. Repeat until chicken is all fried. Place
in a large bowl.

Put 6 cups water in a 12 quart pot. Bring to a boil. Then add

4 lb. celery cut in slices 1/4" thick
2 lb. bamboo shoots rinsed and cut in slices 1/4"x1/4"x2"
4 lb. canned or fresh mushrooms sliced 1/4" thick
4 lb. celery cabbage or Chinese cabbage sliced 1/4" thick
2 lb. onion cut 1/4" thick then in half
1 lb. water chestnuts sliced 1/4" thick
10 envelopes MBT Chicken Bouillon
1/2 teaspoon garlic powder

Bring pot to a boil. Then simmer 5 minutes. Add

1 quart of water
6 tablespoons corn starch
4 tablespoons soy sauce
1/4 cup dry sherry
1 tablespoon sugar
1/8 teaspoon pepper

Stir until sauce thickens. Add chicken and stir. Serve with rice
for Chop Suey, with fried noodles for Chow Mein. This can be
served without any other main dishes except a soup and a
dessert. It is filling and easy to make. It also holds well on a
heated serving tray.

Variations: For Beef Chop Suey or Chow Mein, add 6 lb. flank
steak sliced 1/8 'x2"x1/2" and brown it. Add at the same point
in the recipe as chicken. For Shrimp Chop Suey or Chow Mein,
buy 6 lb. precooked shrimp. Thaw it in cold water and add at
the same time you add the corn starch mixture. The shrimp will
heat up as the sauce thickens without overcooking.

CHICKEN WITH MUSHROOMS

Take 8 lb. raw boned chicken and slice it 1/8"x1"x2".
Fry it 1 lb. at a time with 1 tablespoon peanut oil and 1 clove
garlic minced fine. Cook until chicken turns white. Remove to
large mixing bowl. Repeat until chicken is all fried.

Take 2 lbs. canned mushrooms, stems and pieces, and fry in
1 tablespoon peanut oil 4 minutes. Add to bowl containing
chicken.

Take 1 lb. water chestnuts sliced 1/8" thick and lb. bamboo
shoots, rinsed and cut 1/8"x1"x2". Fry in 1 tablespoon peanut
oil about 4 minutes. Add 2 tablespoons soy sauce and 2
tablespoons dry sherry, and fry for 2 minutes. Add to bowl
containing the chicken and mushrooms.

Place in a 12 quart pot:
2 quarts water
8 envelopes MBT Chicken Bouillon
1/4 teaspoon garlic powder

Bring to a boil. Then add contents of mixing bowl.
Heat 2-3 minutes, then add:

2 cups water
1/2 cup corn starch
2 tablespoons soy sauce

Stir until sauce starts to thicken. Serve with rice.
Each portion is 8 oz.

PEPPER STEAK FOR 25 PEOPLE

Take 6 lb. flank or round steak, firm it in the freezer, then slice it 1/8"x1"x2". Brown the steak in 1 tablespoon of peanut oil in a large wok or frying pan, about 3/4 of a lb. at a time. Repeat until meat is all fried. Place the fried meat in a large bowl or pan in a warm oven.

In a 12 quart pot, heat
6 cups water
4 envelopes MBT Chicken Bouillon or equivalent
2 lbs. onion cut in wedges
3 lb. green peppers cut 1"x1"
2 tablespoons sherry
1 tablespoon sugar
1/8 teaspoon pepper
4 cloves garlic, minced fine

Bring the mixture to a boil and simmer, with a cover, for 5 minutes. Add the beef and stir. Then add

1-1/2 cups water
6 tablespoons corn starch
3 tablespoons thick soy sauce

Stir until sauce thickens. Serve with rice. If you have the time, the dish can be improved by browning the 4 cloves of garlic in a pot with 1 tablespoon peanut oil before adding it to the liquid mixture. There are no seconds figured in this recipe.

8 ounces are allowed for each person. You may want to serve this with rice and egg roll on a plate with 3 partitions. Egg roll goes well with the steak.

MEAT BALLS WITH CABBAGE FOR 25 PEOPLE

8 lb. lean ground beef
1 cup soy sauce
1/2 cup dry sherry
1/4 cup corn starch

Mix the above with your hands and form into small balls about
18 to the lb., walnut size. Place in bottom of a 12 quart pot.
Add 3 quarts of water and cover. Heat until pot starts to simmer.
Allow to simmer 5 minutes, then add 8 lb. cabbage cut in pieces
1"x2". If you have a food slicer, set the gauge for 1" and then
cut slices in 2" strips. Let pot simmer 10-15 minutes more.
Remove meat balls and cabbage with a slotted spoon to heated
serving tray.

Return pot to stove. Bring back to a boil and add

1 cup water
4 envelopes MBT Chicken Bouillon
2 tablespoons soy sauce
1/4 cup corn starch

Mix and cook until sauce starts to thicken. Pour over cabbage
and meatballs in the serving tray. Serve with rice. Each portion
will be about 10 ounces.

This recipe is extremely easy to put together, but the flavor
combination is something very special The sauce picks up the
flavor from the meat. For a variation in flavor, lean pork can
be mixed in with the beef in any proportion. Be sure to simmer
a few extra minutes to cook the pork completely.

SWEET & SOUR MEAT BALLS FOR 25 PEOPLE

8 lb. lean ground beef
8 oz. minced onion
1/2 cup soy sauce
1/4 cup dry sherry
8 oz. water chestnuts minced fine

Mix the above together with your hands and form into small balls about 18 to the pound, walnut size.

Beat 3 eggs. Drop meat balls into egg mixture and roll them around with chopsticks until they are covered with egg. Then roll the balls around on a plate containing 2 cups of corn starch until they are covered with white starch.

Deep fry at 350 degrees until brown. Keep warm in a deep pan in a 250 degree oven.

Place in a large saucepan:

1 quart water
4 envelopes MBT Chicken Bouillon
1 quart wine vinegar
2 cups sugar
1/2 cup catsup
1/2 cup corn starch
1 cup juice from pineapple
1 cup juice from sweet mixed pickles
1/4 cup soy sauce
2 lb. green peppers cut in 1" squares

Heat until sauce becomes thick and translucent. Add

2 lbs. mixed sweet pickles
2 lb. pineapple chunks

Stir and simmer for 3 minutes. Pour over meatballs in oven. Top with 1/2 lb. shredded cocoanut. Serve with rice. This recipe will serve 25, with about 12 oz. per portion.

ROAST PORK FOR 25 PEOPLE

Take 12-14 lbs. of pork butt or loin. Bone it. Trim off the fat, and cut the remaining meat in strips 1" thick, 3" wide, and 6-7" long. Place it a heavy duty plastic bag.

Mix in blender:
1-1/2 tablespoons sugar
1-1/2 tablespoons honey
1 cup soy sauce
3 cloves garlic
1/2 cup dry sherry
1 teaspoon 5 spice, optional
3 tablespoons catsup

Blend for 2 minutes, medium speed. Pour in plastic bag and seal. Turn every few hours to make sure each piece is in touch with the marinade. Place in refrigerator 3 hours minimum or, better, overnight. Place wire racks over 2 baking pans and put 1 cup water in the bottom of each pan to prevent meat from drying out. Place the pork on the racks and roast in a preheated oven at 350 degrees for 30 minutes. Using a pair of metal tongs, transfer the strips of pork from the rack to the dish with the leftover marinade. Roast 30 minutes more. This is easier than basting. When pork is done, cut on angle across grain 1/4" thick and serve with hot mustard or Duck Sauce.
This will make portions of about 8 oz. each. Use this as a side dish or as one item on a 3 compartment plate.

Bibliography

Alexander, Helen. Hawaiian Cookbook, Hawaiian Service, 1947.
American Home Econ. Assoc., The World's Favorite Recipes From The
    U.N., Harper & Row, 1951.
Armitage, Merle. Fit For A King, Longmans, 1939.
Army Language School Women's Club. What's Cooking Around The
    World, 1953.
Au, M. Sing. The Chinese Cookbook, Culinary Arts, 1966.
Bazore, Katherine. Hawaiian & Pacific Foods, Barrows, 1940.
Beilenson, Edna. Simple Hawaiian Cookery, Peter Pauper Press, 1964.
Beilenson, Edna. Simple Oriental Cookery, Peter Pauper Press, 1960.
Benedictine Sisters of Peking. The Art of Chinese Cooking, Tuttle, 1966.
Be-Sing, Hsu. How To Be An Expert in Chinese Cooking Without Even
    Trying, Vantage Press, 1972.
Body, Ann. The Gourmet Guide To Chinese Cooking, Derbibooks, 1975.
Body, Ann. Chinese Cooking, Octopus, 1974.
Brissenden, Rosemary. South-East Asian Food, Penguin Books, 1969.
Brobeck, Florence. Cooking With Curry, Barrows, 1952.
Brunner, Louscne. Casserole Treasury, Harper & Row, 1964.
Buck, Pearl. Oriental Cookbook, Simon & Schuster, 1972.
Bunn, Mrs. Secrets From Peking, Bun-BMP Publishing, no date.
Burke, Helen. Chinese Cooking For Pleasure, Hamlyn, 1965.
Burt, Alison. Popular Chinese Cookery, Octopus, 1972.
Burt, Elinor. Far Eastern Cookery, Little, Brown & Co., 1947.
Caleva, Harry. Chinese Cookbook For Quantity Service, Ahrens, 1958.
Campbell, Elizabeth. Encyl. Of World Cookery, Spring Books, no date.
Carrier. International Cookery Cards (China), Nelson, 1969.
Chan, Ester. Chinese Cookery Secrets, Chungtai Press, 1960.
Chan, Shiu Wong. The Chinese Cookbook, Stokes, 1917.
Chan, Sou. House of Chan Cookbook, Doubleday & Co., 1952.
Chan, Titus. The Chan-Ese Way, Reston Publishing Co., 1974.
Chang, Constance. Chinese Cooking 1, Shufunotomo, 1968.
Chang, Constance. Chinese Cooking 2, Shufunotomo, 1968.
Chang, Constance. Chinese Party Book, Nelson, 1972.
Chang, Constance. Full Color Chinese Cooking, Shufunotomo, 1969.
Chang, Constance. Quick and Easy Chinese Cooking, Shufunotomo, 1969.
Chang, Isabelle Chin. Gourmet On The Go, Tuttle, 1970.
Chang, Isabelle. What's Cooking at the Changs, Liveright, 1959
Chang, Wonona & Irving B. Encyl. of Chinese Food & Cooking, Crown, 1970.
Chang, Wonona & Kutcher, Austin. Northern Chinese Cookbook.
Chao, Buwei Yang. How to Cook & Eat in Chinese, Random House, 1963.
Chao, Buwei Yang. How to Eat in A Chinese Restaurant, Vintage, 1974.

Char, Alyce & Theodore Char. The Gourmet's Encyl. of Chinese-Hawaiian Cooking, Exposition Press, 1972.

Chen, Joyce. Joyce Chen Cookbook, Lippencott, 1962.

Cheng, F.T. Musings of A Chinese Gourmet, Hutchinson Publishing Co., 1954.

Cheng, Julia Chih. Chinese Home Cooking, Kodansha, 1972.

Cheng, S.K. Shanghai Restaurant Cookbook, 1936.

Chi, Yuan-Shan Huang. Chinese Gourmet, Book World, 1961.

Chiang, Cecilia S. The Mandarin Way, Little, Brown & Co., 1974.

Chiang, Mme. Mei-Ling. Madam Chiangs Cookbook, Chinese Book Co., 1941.

Chih, Chuang Shu. Chinese Health Foods, Shufunotomo, 1972.

Chinese Cooking Companions. Chop Suey a la Carte, Japan Publications, 1966.

Cho Ong-Ok, Cho. The Art of Korean Cookery, Shibita, 1963.

Chou, Eric. Chinese Cooking The Easy Way, Miniby Corgi, 1972.

Chow, Dolly. (C.T. Wang) Chow! Secrets of Chinese Cooking, Tuttle, 1965.

Choy, Jung Suck. The Art of Oriental Cooking, Ward Ritchie, 1964.

*Chu, Grace Z. Madame Chu's Chinese Cooking School, S&S, 1975.

*Chu, Grace Z. The Pleasures of Chinese Cooking, Simon & Schuster, 1962.

Chun, Lee To. Chinese Cooking, Round the World Books, 1973.

Claiborne, Craig. The Chinese Cookbook, Lippencott, 1972.

Claiborne, Craig. The N.Y. Times Cookbook, Harper & Row, 1971.

Clifford, William. The Insiders Guide To Chinese Restaurants in N.Y., Grosset & Dunlap, 1970.

Collier, Patrica. How You Can Give Hawaiian Parties, Dole, no date.

Crascent. The Complete Book of World Cookery, Crescent Books, 1972.

Davis, Lucille. The Court Dishes of China, Tuttle, 1966.

Delfs, Robert. Good Food Of Szechwan, Kodansha, 1974.

Doi, Masuru. Japanese One Pot Cookery, Kodansha, 1970.

Donovan, Maria Kozslik. The Far Eastern Epicure, Doubleday & co., 1958.

*Dorn, Frank. The Dorn Cookbook, Henry Regnery, 1953.

Dorsey, Helen. The Shangri-la Cookbook, Lancer, 1973.

Fang, John T.C. Chinatown Handy Guide, Chinese Publishing House, 1958.

*Farr, Barbara. Wok Cookbook, Pyramid, 1971.

Feng, Doreen Yen Hung. The Joy of Chinese Cooking, Grosset & Dunlap, 1954.

Fitzgerald, Don. Hawaii Cookbook, Pacifica House, 1971.

Flash Books. Exciting Meals Around the World, 1968.

Fortin, Stanley. World Book of Pork Dishes, Pelham, 1967.

Froud, Nina. Cooking the Chinese Way, Spring Books, 1960.

Froud, Nina. Cooking the Japanese Way, Spring Books, 1963.

Froud, Nina. Far Eastern Cooking For Pleasure, Hamlyn, 1971.

Gary. Pacific Hostess Cookbook, Coward-McCann, 1956.

Gebhard, Mary Lou & Butler, William H. Pineapples Passion Fruit & Poi, Tuttle, 1967.

George. Chinese Cooking Manuscript Silversprings, Md., 1970.
Gibbs, Lorene Campbell. Popular Chinese Cookbook, Haldeman.
Gin, Margret & Alfred Castel. Regional Cooking of China, One Hundred One Products, 1975.
Grand Hotel Recreation Club. Chinese Cooking Classes, 1964.
Grossman, Bob & Ruth. The Kosher Cookbook Trilogy, C.I.F. Ericksson, 1965.
Hahn, Emily. The Cooking of China, Time-Life, 1968.
Hatano, Sumi. Homestyle Chinese Cooking in Pictures, Japan Publications, 1975.
Heriteau, Jacqueline. Oriental Cooking the Fast Wok Way, Hawthorn Books, 1971.
Hiang, Lie Sek. Indonesian Cookery, Crown, 1963.
Hilo Woman's Club. Hawaiian Recipes, Hilo Tribune Herald.
Hing, Lei Wai. Chop Suey, Chinese Aid, 1940.
Ho, Lucy. Authentic Chinese Cooking, Dover, 1973.
Hodgson, Moira. Chinese Cooking With American Meals, Doubleday & Co., 1970.
Hong Kong YWCA. Noodles & Rice & Everything Nice, South China Morning Post, 1965.
Hong, Wallace Yee. The Chinese Cookbook, Crown, 1963.
Howe, Robin. Far Eastern Cookery, IWFS, 1969.
Hsu, Rebecca. Gas Cookery Book, Hong Kong & China Gas Co., 1964.
Huang, Leon. Chinese Recipes, Fortune, 1965.
Huang, Paul. The Illustrated Step-By-Step Chinese Cookbook, S&S, 1975.
Ito, Stella. Sukiyaki, New Japanese American News, 1964.
Jackson, Lenli. 100 Simple Chinese Recipes, Saphrograph, 1958.
Jan, Lee Su. The Fine Art of Chinese Cooking, Gramercy, 1962.
Japanese Cooking Companions. Practical Japanese Cooking, Japan Publications, 1967.
Japanese Cooking Companions. Tempura & Sukiyaki, Japan Publications, 1961.
Japanese Cooking Companions. Teriyaki & Sushi, Japan Publications, 1967.
Japan Trade Center. Japanese Recipes, no date.
Kagawa, Aya. Japanese Cookbook, Japan Travel Bureau, 1949.
Kan, Johnny. Eight Immortal Flavors (Secrets of Chinese Cooking), Howell North, 1964.
Kaufman, William I. Oriental Cookery, Centaur House, 1969.
Kaufman, William I. Recipes From the Far East & Near East, Laurel, 1969.
Kaufman, William I. The Wonderful World of Cooking, Laurel, 1964.
Kay, Tutu. The New Wiki Wiki Kau Kau, Kay, 1964.
Keys, John D. Food For the Emperor, Grammercy, 1963.
Kirshman, Irena. Wok & Tempura Cookery, Potpouri Press, 1969.
Kruse, Mary. Round the World Low Calorie Diet Cookbook, Merit, 1969.
Kuo-Shung, Huang. Chinese Cooking Cantonese Style, Jimmys Service, Kin Ma, 1962.
Kwon, George I. Oriental Culinary Art, Kwon, 1933.

Laas, William. Cuisines of the Eastern World, Golden Press 1967.
Lamb Corrinne. Chinese Festive Board, Vetch & Lee, 1970.
Lau, Margret. Chinese Cooking With M.L. Hilo, Herald Tribune, 1962.
Lawson, Helen. How To Make Good Curries, Hamlyn, 1970.
*Lee, Beverly. Easy Way To Chinese Cooking, Doubleday & Co., 1963.
Lee, Calvin. Chinese Cooking for American Kitchens, Putnam, 1958.
Lee, Calvin & Lee, Audry. Regional Chinese Cooking, Putnam, 1975.
Lee, Gary. Chinese Tasty Tales Cookbook, O'Hara, 1974.
Lee, Garry. The Chinese Vegetarian Cookbook, Nitty Gritty, 1972.
Lee, Garry. The Wok, a Chinese Cookbook, Nitty Gritty, 1970.
Lee, Helen Chiang. A Chinese Cookbook for Everyone, Exposition Press, 1962.
Lee, Jim. Chinese Cookbook, Harper & Row, 1968.
Lee, M.P. Chinese Cookery, Transatlantic, 1945.
Lem, Arthur. Hong Kong Cookbook, F&W, 1970.
Lew & Lee. Peking Table Top Cooking, Gala, 1972.
Li, Hsu Ying. His Favorite Cookbook, Valid, 1974.
Lin, Chan Sow. Chinese Party Book, 1963.
Lin, Chan Sow. Chinese Restaurant Dishes, Marican & Sons, 1958.
Lin, Chan Sow. 75 Chinese Restaurant Dishes, Book 2, 1960.
Lin, Florence. Florence Lin's Chinese Regional Cookbook, Hawthorn, 1975.
Lin, Hsiangju & Tsuifeng. Secrets of Chinese Cooking, Prentice Hall, 1960.
Lin, Tsuifeng & Hsiangju. Chinese Gastronomy, Hastings House, 1969.
Ling, Mei-Mei. Chop Suey, Chop Suey, 1953.
Liu, William T. The Essence of Chinese Food, Aurora Pubs., 1970.
Lo, Kenneth. Chinese Food, Penguin, 1972.
Lo, Kenneth. The Chinese Vegetarian Cookbook, Pantheon, 1974.
Lo, Kenneth. Cooking The Chinese Way, Acro, 1963.
Lo, Kenneth. Peking Cooking, Faber, 1971.
Lo, Kenneth. Quick & Easy Chinese Cooking, Houghton Mifflin, 1972.
Long, How. Chinese Chop Suey, Woh Long & Co., 1924.
Low, Henry. Cook at Home in Chinese, Pacific Printing, no date.
Ma, Ma etc. Don't Lick The Chopsticks, Kodansha, 1973.
Marsh, Dorothy. The Good Housekeeping International Cookbook, Harcourt, 1964.
Ma, Mrs. Mrs. Ma's Favorite Chinese Recipes, Kodansha, 1968.
*Ma, Nancy Chih. Mrs. Ma's Chinese Cookbook, Tuttle, 1965.
*Ma, Nancy Chih. Cook Chinese, Kodansha, 1967.
*Mecklenburg, K.K. Cook Polynesian, 1968.
Mei, Anna Kong. Chinese Rice Bowl, Mercury, 1943.
Mei, Pei. Chinese Cookbook, Tiwan, 1969.
Mei, Yu Wen. 100 Most Honorable Chinese Recipes, Crowell, 1963.
Miller, Bazore, Bartow. Fruits of Hawaii, Univ. of Hawaii, 1955.
Miller, Gloria Bley. The Thousand Recipe Chinese Cookbook, Atheneum, 1966.
Min, Chan Kan. Practical Chinese Cooking, Japan Publications, 1969.

214

Min, Chen Jian. Typical Chinese Cooking, Japan Publications, 1970.
Min, Rebecca, Hsu Hui. The Delights of Chinese Cooking, Prentice Hall, 1971.
Mitchell, Alice Miller. Oriental Cookbook, Rand McNally, 1954.
Morphy, Countess. Recipes of All Nations, Wise, 1935.
Morgan, H.T. Food the Chinese Way or 30 Tested Recipes, 1940.
Morris, Harriett. The Art Of Korean Cooking, Tuttle, 1960.
Namba, Ayako. Chinese Cooking ABC, Shufunotomo, 1973.
O'Brien, Eileen. Hawaiian Host & Hostess Book, Tong, 1969.
Oliver, Frank. Chinese Cooking, Deutch, 1955.
Ouei, Mimie. The Art of Chinese Cooking, Random House, 1960.
Pacific Trading Co. Mandarin Chop Suey Book, 1928.
Parker, Netta. The Home Book of Oriental Cookery, Farber, 1966.
Piper, M.R. Oriental Cookbook, Sunset, 1970.
Quan. Chinese Recipes, Quan Quan, 1942.
Reejhsinghani, Aroona. Housewifes Guide to Chinese Cooking, Jaico Pub., 1972.
Richards, Charles & Janet. Basic Chinese & Japanese Recipes, City Lights, 1958.
Richmond, Sonya. The Art of Chinese Cookery, Foyles, 1964.
Rook, Ethel Moore. Chinese Recipes, Doubleday & Co., 1923.
Rosen, Ruth C. Ancestral Recipes of Shen Mei Lon, Rosen, 1954.
Rosen, Ruth C. Nippon These, Rosen, 1961.
Rosenbaum, Helen. Everything You Wanted to Know about Chinese Food, Signette, 1971.
Ross, Irma Walker. Recipes From the East, Tuttle, 1968.
Rubin, Cynthia & Jerome. Cooking: Chinese, Emporium, 1975.
Schafer, C & V. Wokcraft, Yerba Buena Press, 1972.
Schryver, Alice. Oriental Cooking, Grossert, 1975.
Searle, Townley. Strange News From China, E.P. Dutton.
Shimizu, Kay. Asian Flavors, Exposition, 1972.
Shinojima, Tadashi. Japanese Cookery 20 Recipes, Shufunotomo, 1968.
Shinojima, Tadashi. Japanese Cooking, Cards, Shufunotomo, 1966.
Sia, Mary. Chinese Cookbook, Univ. of Hawaii, 1967.
Sis, Vladimir. Chinese Food & Fables, Artia, 1966.
Small, Marvin. The Worlds Best Recipes, Pocket Books, 1957.
Smith, Gladys. Chop Suey, Chinese Aid, Boston, 1940.
Smith, Herman. Kitchens Near & Far, Barrows, 1945.
Solomon, Charmaine. Chinese Cookbook, Hamlyn, 1973.
Solomon, Charmaine. Far Eastern Cookbook, Hamlyn, 1972.
Spira, Ruth. Naturally Chinese: Healthful Cooking From China, Rodale, 1974.
Spunt, Georges. The Step by Step Chinese Cookbook, Crowell, 1973.
Stallard, Louise. Cooking Hunan Style, Drake, 1973.
Stallard, Louise. Cooking Szechuan Style, Drake, 1973.
Steinberg, Rafael. Pacific & Southeast Asia Cooking, Time-Life, 1970.
Steiner, Andrew Hen-Lee. Chinese Cooking, Bonjour Press.

Suitin, L. Choice Chinese Cookery, Asia Pacific, 1969.
Tada, Tatsuji. Japanese Recipes, Tuttle, 1970.
Tai, Pauline. The Bachelorette Cookbook, Doubleday & Co., 1968.
Tested Recipe Institute. Chinese Cookery, Grosset & Dunlap.
Tiwan, Republic of China. The Art of Chinese Cooking.
Tong, Gee Nee. Chopsticks Unlimited of New Orleans, Pelican, 1969.
Tongg. The Hawaiian Homemakers Favorite Island Recipes, Tongg Pub.,
    1956.
Tongg. Japanese & Chinese Recipes, Tongg Pub., 1961.
*Toupin, Elizabeth. Hawaii Cookbook & Back Yard Luau, Bantam, 1967.
*Toupin, Elizabeth. Restaurant of the 5 Volcanos, 1964.
Tove. Simple Chinese Cookery, Peter Pauper Press, 1972.
Trent, May Wong. Fifty Precious Chinese Recipes, Macmillan, 1973
Tseng, Rosy. Chinese Cooking Made Easy, Tuttle, 1967.
Tuan, Willie. The Wok Way, Owlswood, 1974.
Tuttle. Hawaiian Cuisine, Tuttle, 1963.
Vic, Trader. Trader Vic's Book of Food & Drink, Doubleday & Co., 1946.
Vic, Trader. Trader Vic's Pacific Island Cookbook, Doubleday & Co., 1968.
Waldo, Myra. Myra Waldo's Chinese Cookbook, Macmillan, 1968.
Waldo, Myra. The Complete Book of Oriental Cooking, Bantam, 1960.
Waldo, Myra. The Round the World Cookbook, Bantam, 1954.
Wang, Mrs. Linda. Illustrated Chinese Cookbook, Kamakura, 1971.
Waseda, Eisaku. Notes on Japanese Cuisine, 1946.
William, Ann. Grande Diplome Cooking Course: No. 48 Chinese Cooking,
    Purnell, 1972.
Wilson, Christine. Secrets of Eastern Cooking, Hastings House, 1966.
Wilson, Trevor. Great Rice Dishes of the World, Smith, 1970.
*Wing, Fred. New Chinese Recipes, Edelmuth, 1963.
Womans Day. Womans Day International Collectors Cookbook, Fawcett,
    1967.
Womens Society First Methodist Church. Kau-Kau Keepsake Kook Book
Womens Society of St. Marks Church. Treasured Recipes from 2 Cultures,
    A&C, 1969.
Wong, Ella-Mei. Chinese Cookery, Acro, 1961.
Wong, Gail. From Hawaii Authentic-Original Chinese Recipes, I. Wong,
    1966.
Wong, Hi-Ton. Chinese Recipes with Demonstrative Pictures, no. pub. given.
Wong, Hi-Ton. Chinese Recipes:
    Book 1. Appetizers
    Book 2. Pork and Beef
    Book 3. Seafood
    Book 4. Eggs & Vegetables
    Book 5. Soups & Dim Sums, no pub. given.
Wong, Richard. Enjoy Chinese Cooking at Home, Mon Fong Wo, 1949.
Wong, Tyrus. Gourmet Celestial, The L.A. Chinese Womens Club, 1970.
*Wu, Madame. Art of Chinese Cooking, Charles Pub., 1973.

Yang, Kuang-Teh. 50 Chinese Recipes, Saphrograph, 1964.
Yao, James C. Chinese Cuisine Made Easy, 1972.
Yee, Lannie King. Lets Cook The Chinese Way, Tuttle, 1973.
Yee, Rhoda. Chinese Village Cookbook, Yerba Buena Press, 1975.
Young, Grace H. Culinary Road to China, Union County Times, 1967.
Young, Myrtle Lum. Fun With Chinese Recipes, Vantage Books, 1958.
Young, Patrica. Ko Chai's Chinese Kitchen, K&W, 1972.
Yung, Li. Chinese Recipes & Cooking, Wan Li Books, 1973.
Yung, Li. Chinese Refreshment, Wan Li Books, 1973.
*Yung, Victor Sen. The Great Wok Cookbook, Nash, 1974.
Zobel, Myron. Global Cuisine, Patron Press.

*means that the book is recommended.

Index

220

221

For a catalog of other books from The Bess Press, write to

The Bess Press
P. O. Box 22388
Honolulu, HI 96823